SAN FRANCISCO
From The Ground Up

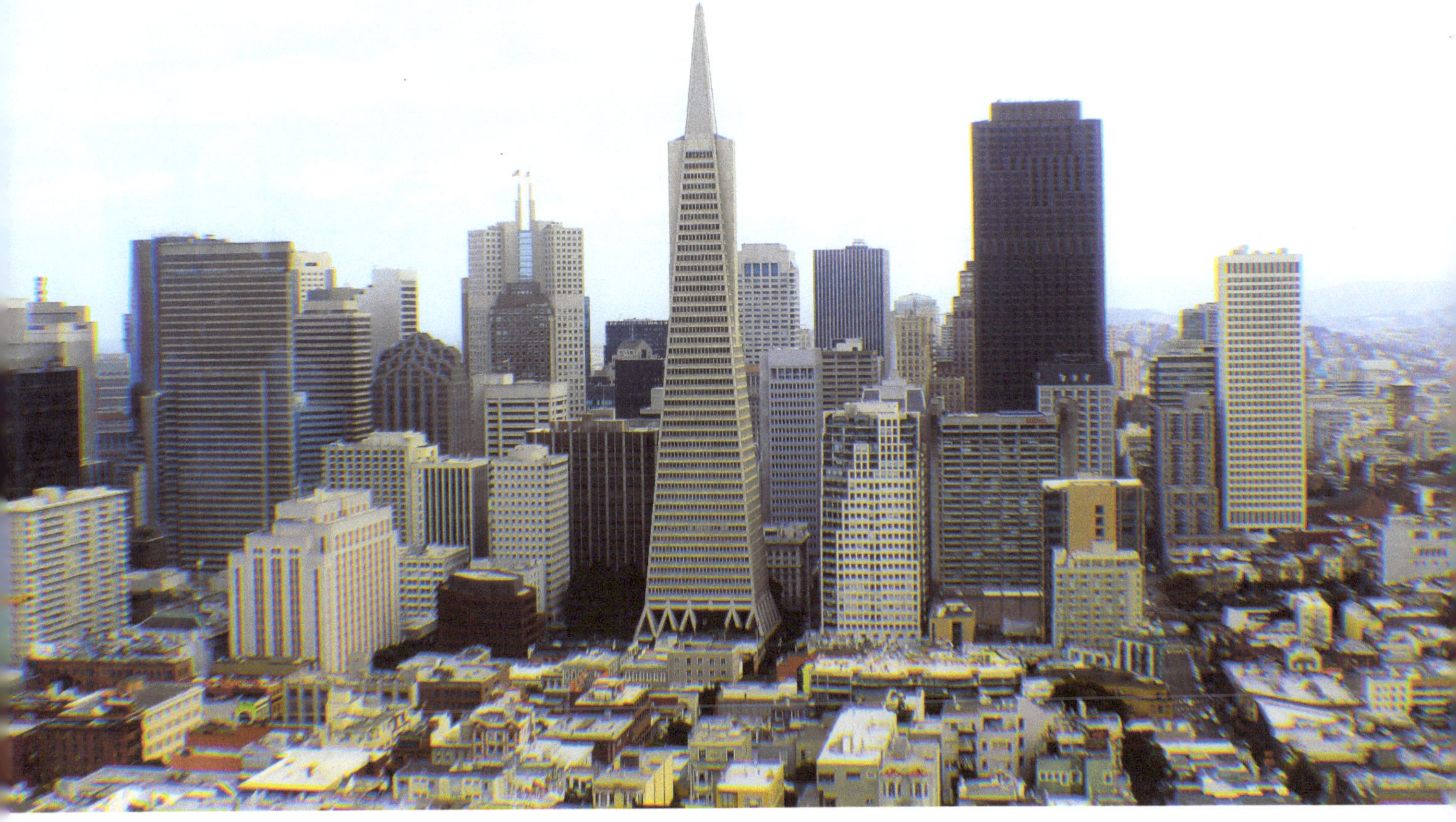

Salvadore Newton

ISBN: 1482663201

ISBN 13: 9781482663204

Library of Congress Control Number: 2013905397

CreateSpace Independent Publishing Platform

North Charleston, South Carolina

IN MEMORY OF JOEL HOWARD CONKLIN

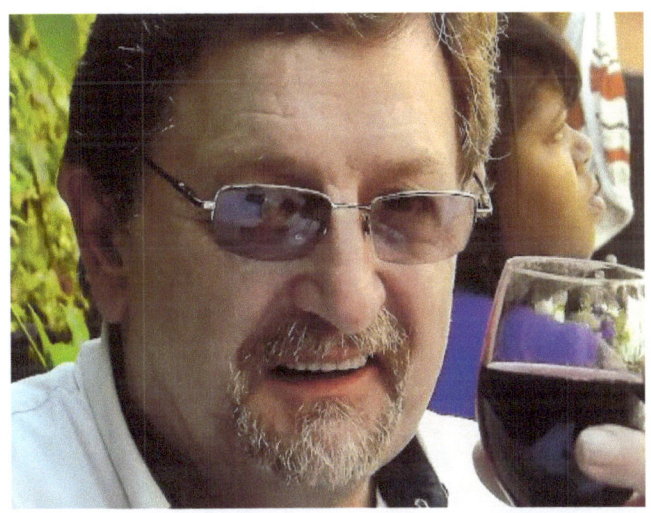

This book is dedicated to my friend Joel Howard Conklin. Tragically, before this project could be finished, Joel lost his battle with cancer. Joel loved art, especially photography; because of this, I have included in this book a special section that displays some of Joel's photographic artwork. When Joel and I set off to complete this project he made me promise that, should he not survive, I would see it through to the end. Now, more than a year later, I am finally able to keep that promise. Joel, I hope that this book has become all that you had hoped for.

Cheers!

ACKNOWLEDGMENTS

Joel and I would like to thank Sheila and Richard Newton, Andrea and David Morgan, Cindy Torres-Rica, Kevin Silva, Christopher Shaw, my wife Diana and son Hunter for their patience and understanding during the completion of this project, and the Create Space Team. Their assistance was vital to this project's success.

I would also like to thank my friend Joel Howard Conklin, for his friendship and knowledge of photography. Through his mentorship I discovered a love of photography that I never knew I had. God bless you Joel, you will be missed by all who had the honor of knowing you.

SAN FRANCISCO

From the Ground Up

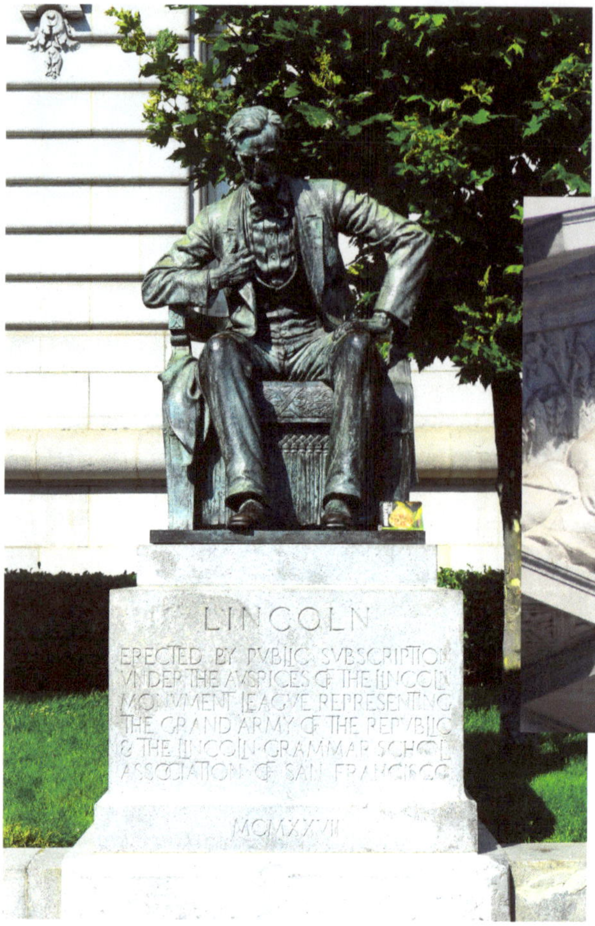

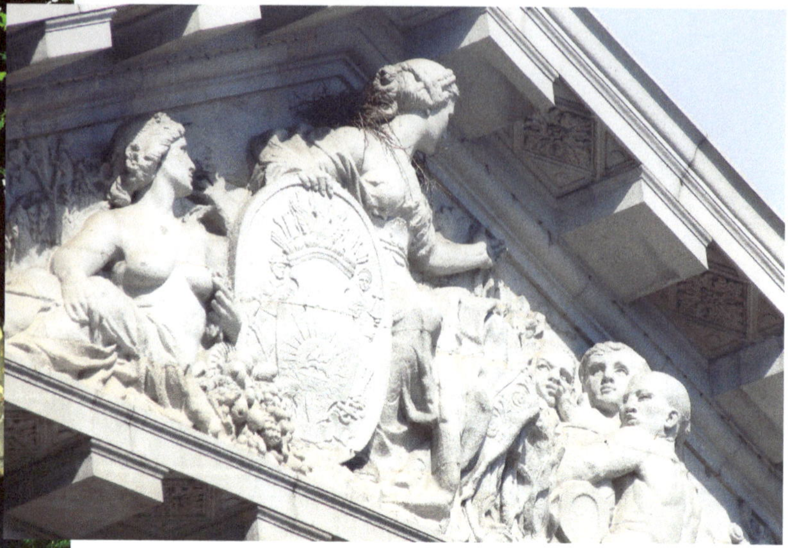

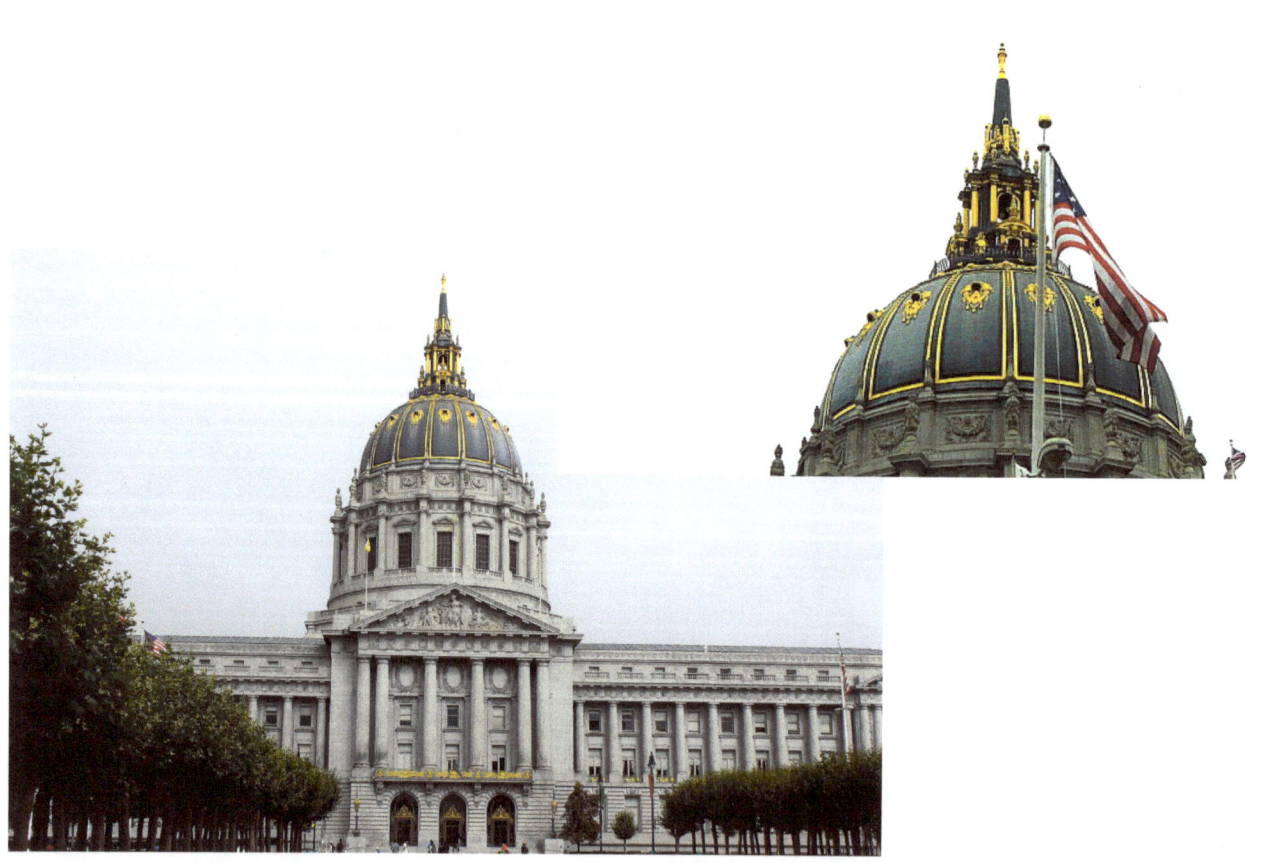

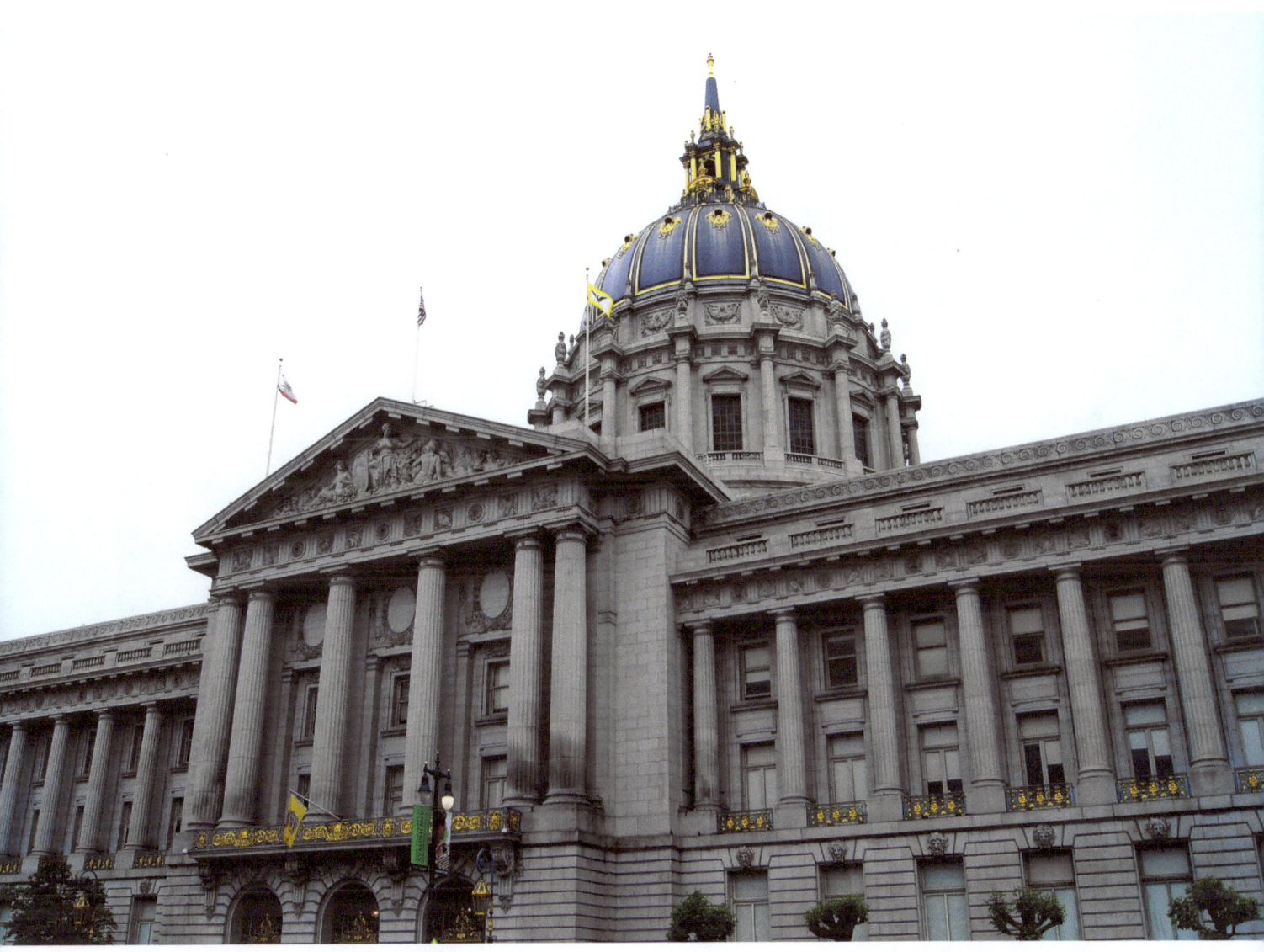

CITY HALL

Rebuilt after the 1906 earthquake, San Francisco City Hall was completed in 1915, three years after construction began, for a total cost of $3.4 million. Designed by architects Bakewell and Brown, the structure boasts a granite exterior, and an interior of Indiana Sandstone, California Marble and Manchurian Oak. City Hall has the fifth largest dome in the world and with a height of 307.5 feet (93.73 meters), 4 floors and a total area of over 550,000 square feet (more than 46,000 square meters), San Francisco City Hall is quite a spectacle to behold.

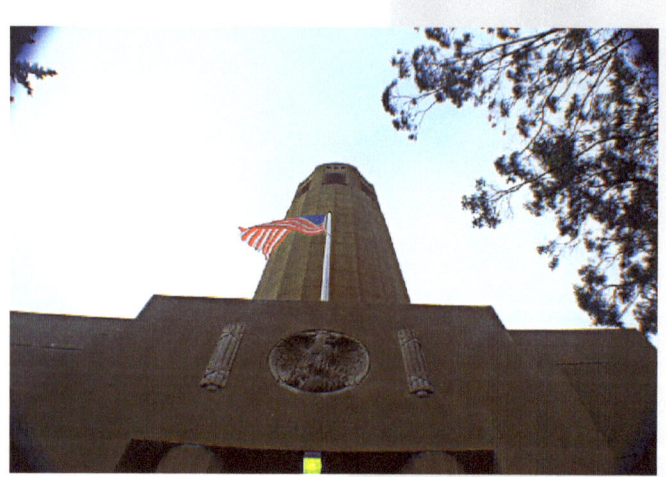

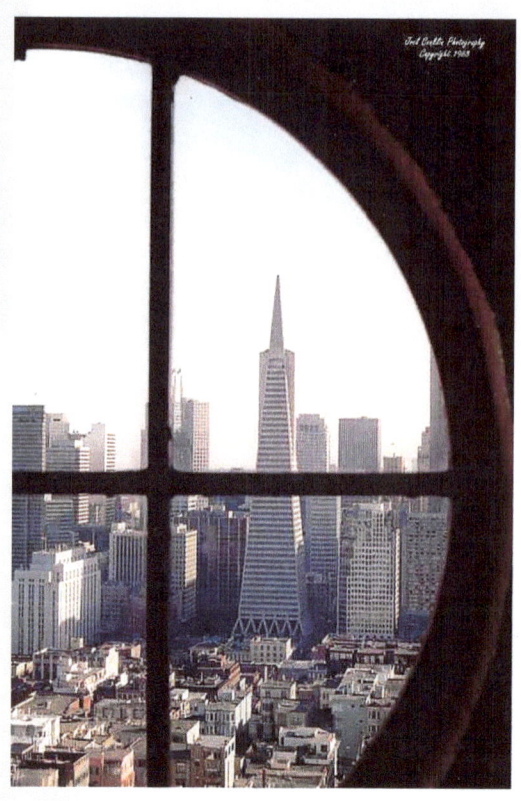

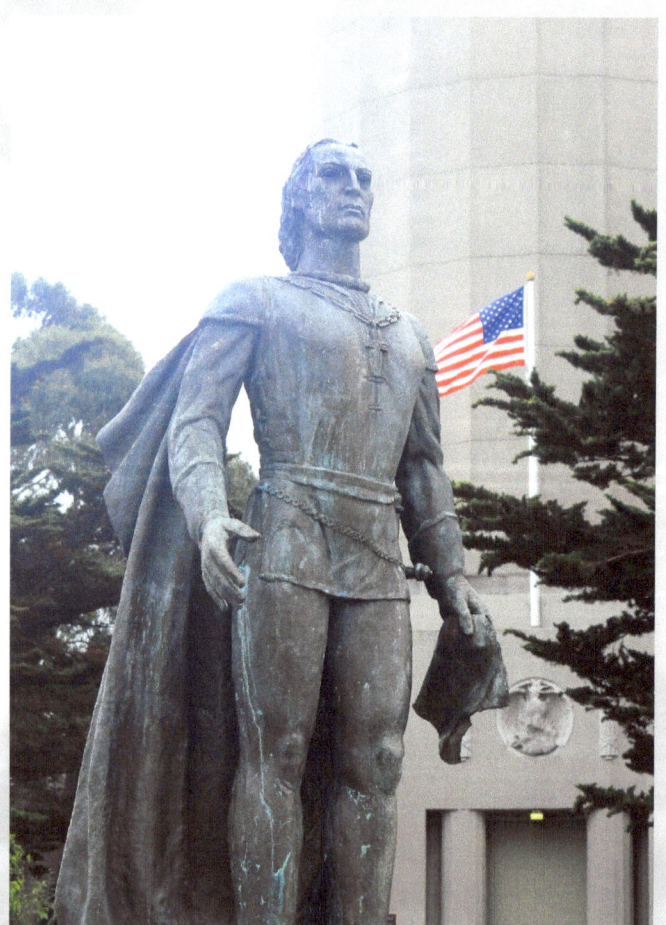

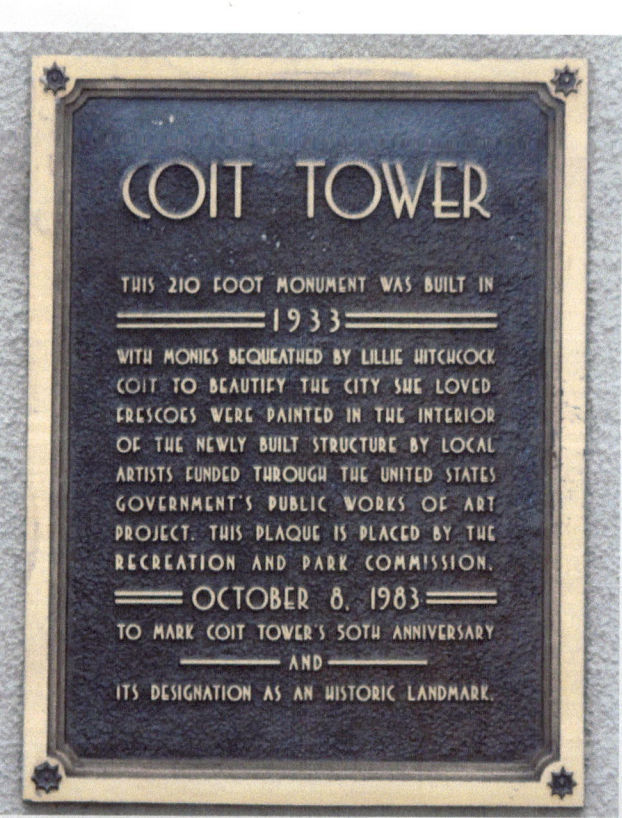

COIT TOWER

THIS 210 FOOT MONUMENT WAS BUILT IN

1933

WITH MONIES BEQUEATHED BY LILLIE HITCHCOCK COIT TO BEAUTIFY THE CITY SHE LOVED FRESCOES WERE PAINTED IN THE INTERIOR OF THE NEWLY BUILT STRUCTURE BY LOCAL ARTISTS FUNDED THROUGH THE UNITED STATES GOVERNMENT'S PUBLIC WORKS OF ART PROJECT. THIS PLAQUE IS PLACED BY THE RECREATION AND PARK COMMISSION.

OCTOBER 8, 1983

TO MARK COIT TOWER'S 50TH ANNIVERSARY

AND

ITS DESIGNATION AS AN HISTORIC LANDMARK.

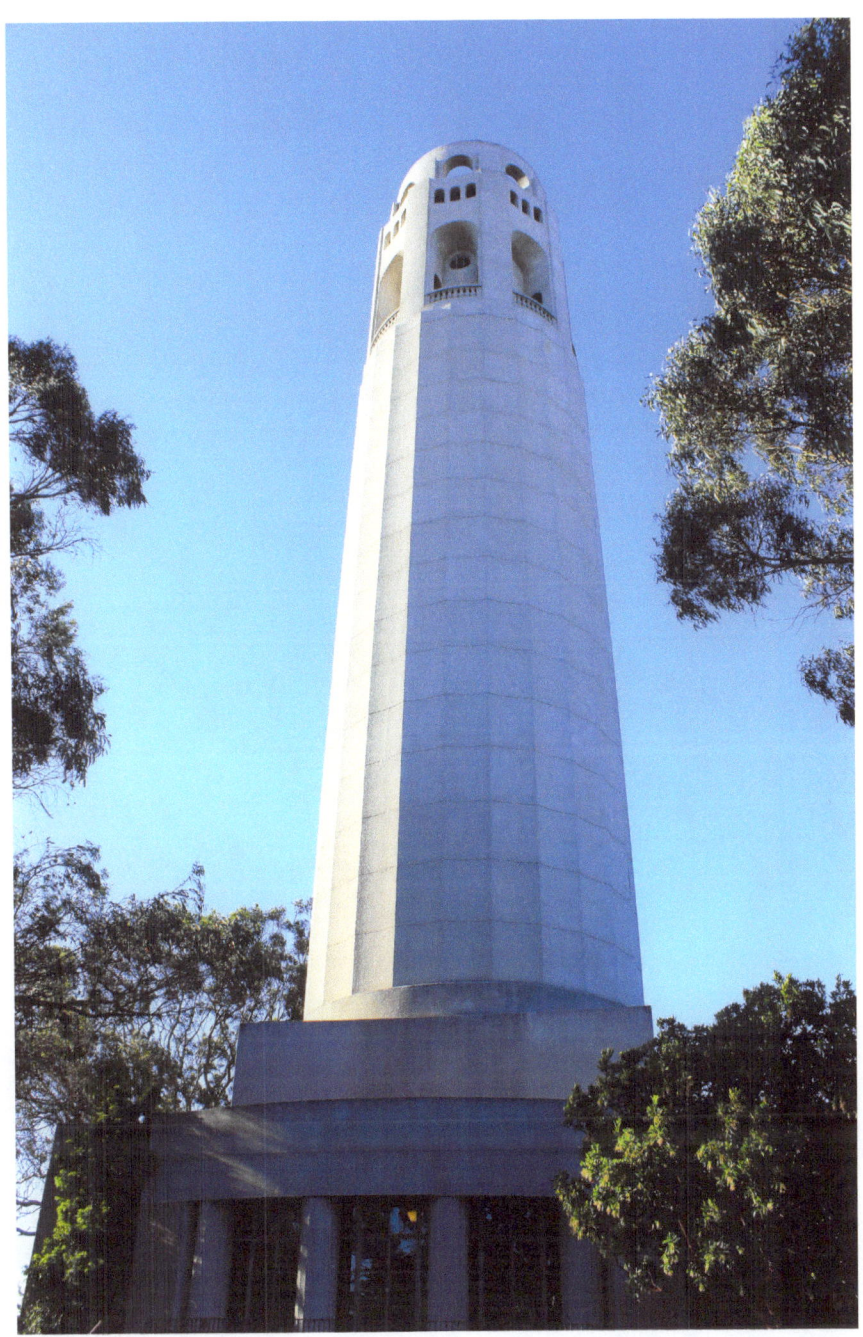

COIT TOWER

Located on top of Telegraph Hill, Coit Tower is a prominent landmark in San Francisco. The tower was constructed in 1933 to honor the volunteer firemen who gave their lives defending San Francisco. Architect Arthur Brown Jr. designed the tower to be constructed of unpainted reinforced concrete. Coit Tower contains multiple murals, and an observation deck that visitors can reach by elevator or stairs. With a height of 210 feet (64 meters), Coit Tower provides an excellent observation point above the city of San Francisco.

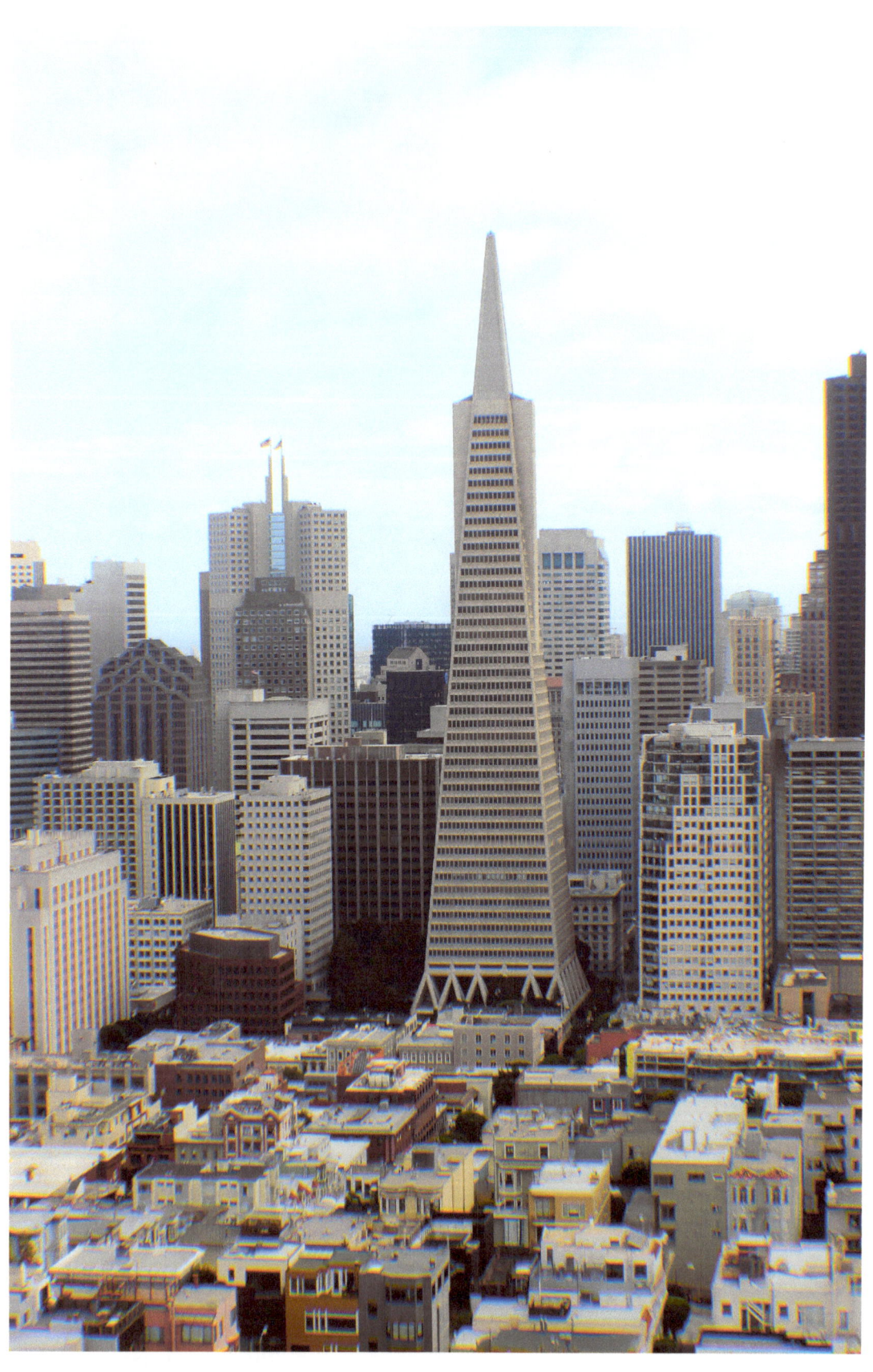

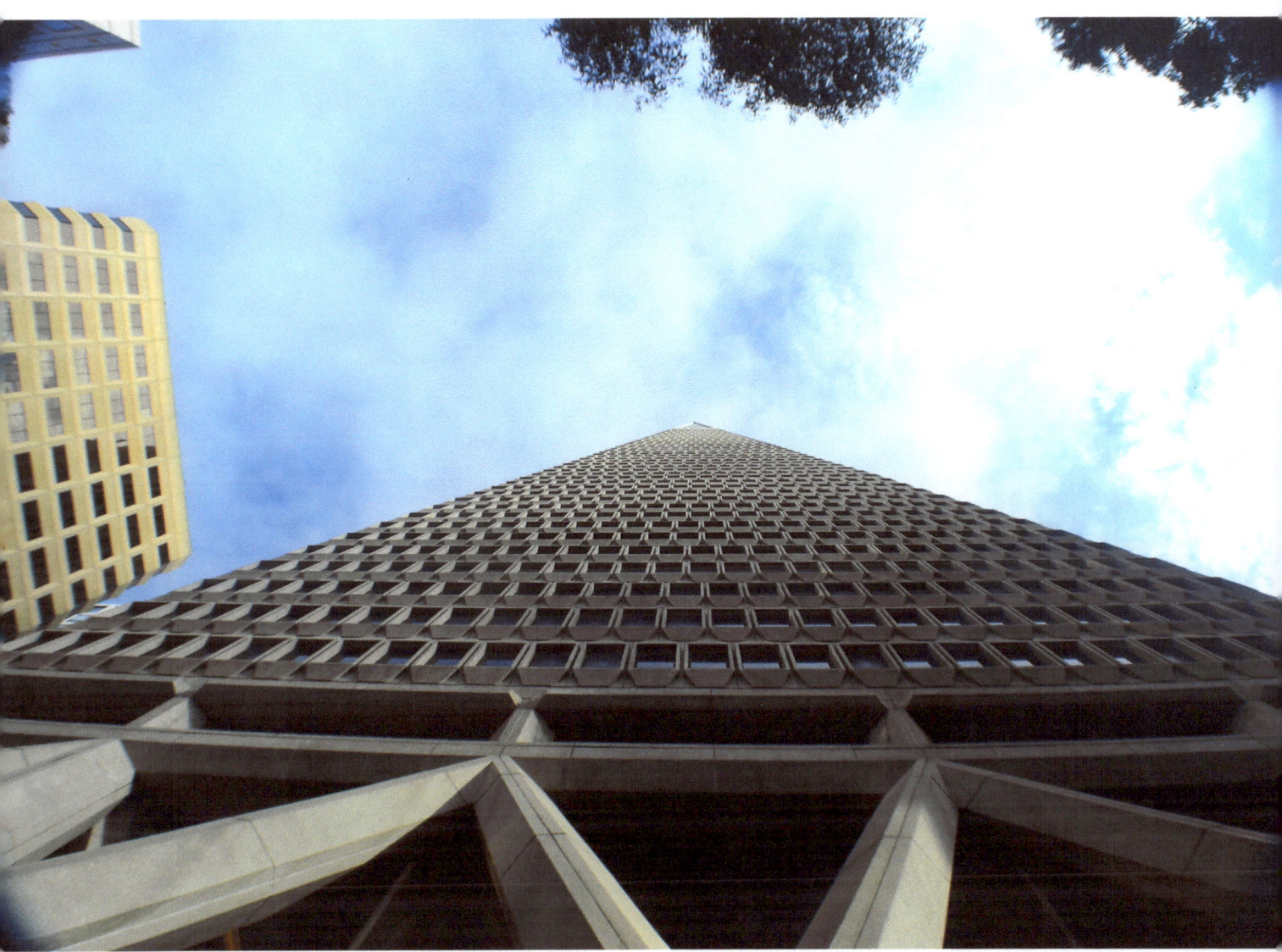

TRANSAMERICA BUILDING

Designed by architect William L. Pereira, the Transamerica Building is an iconic landmark in the city of San Francisco. Towering over the financial district with a total height of 853 feet (260 meters), the Transamerica Building contains 48 floors for a total of 530,000 square feet (49,000 square meters). Construction of the building was completed in 1972; it's base is 4 stories high and contains 16,000 cubic yards (12,000 cubic meters) of concrete, reinforced with 300 miles (480 kilometers) of steel rebar. The Transamerica contains 3,678 windows and is used for office space.

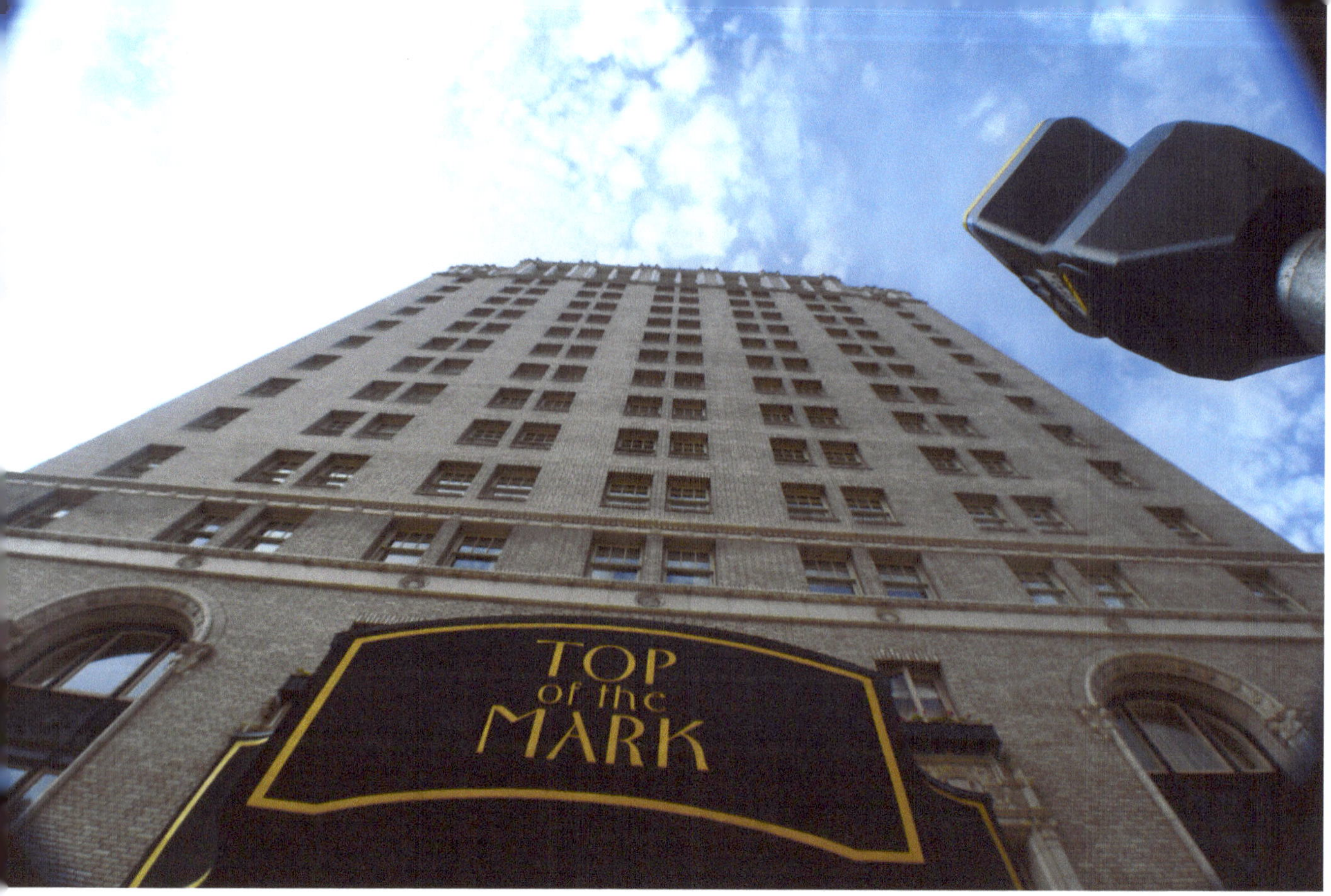
TOP
of the
MARK

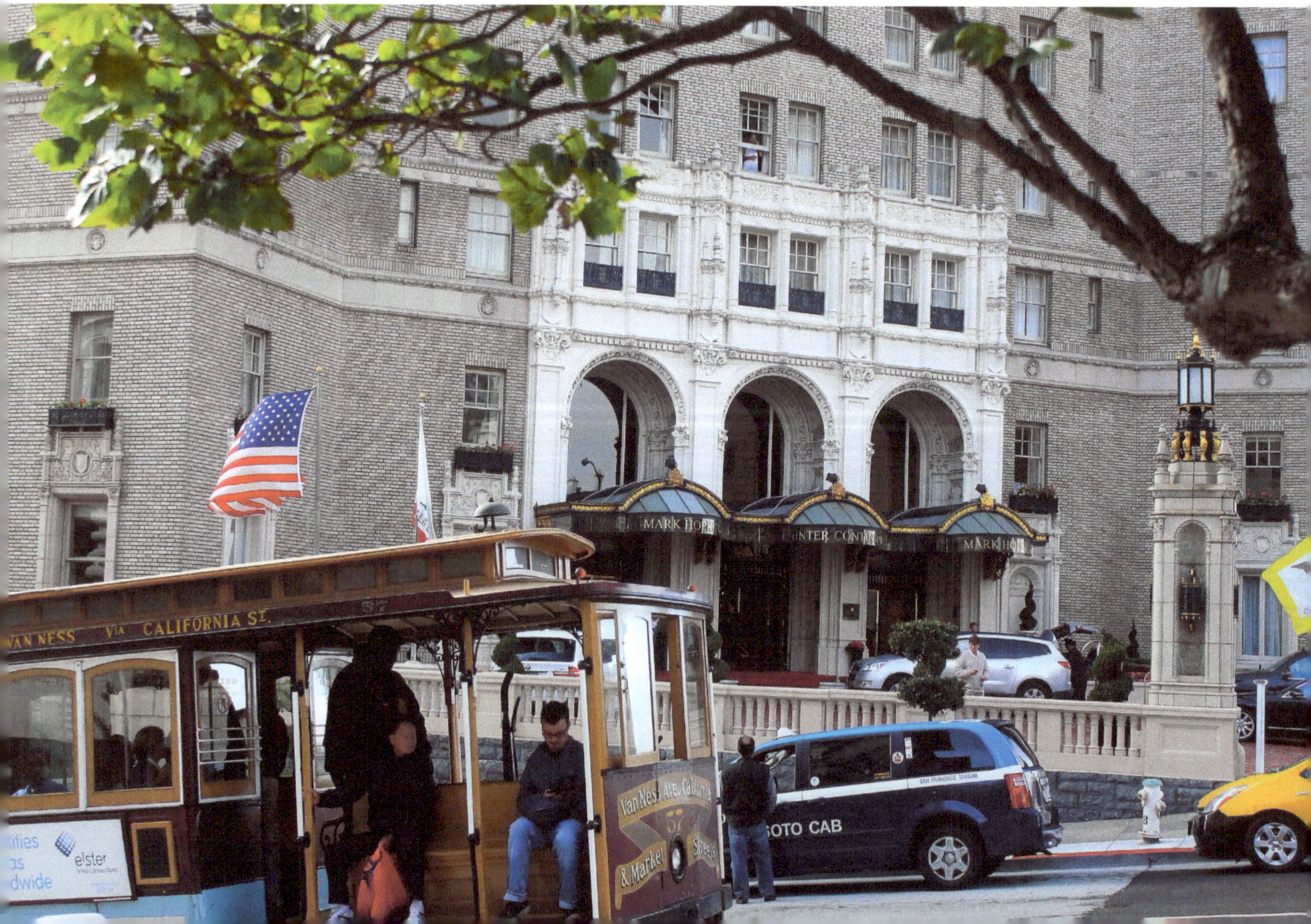
VIA CALIFORNIA ST.
SOTO CAB

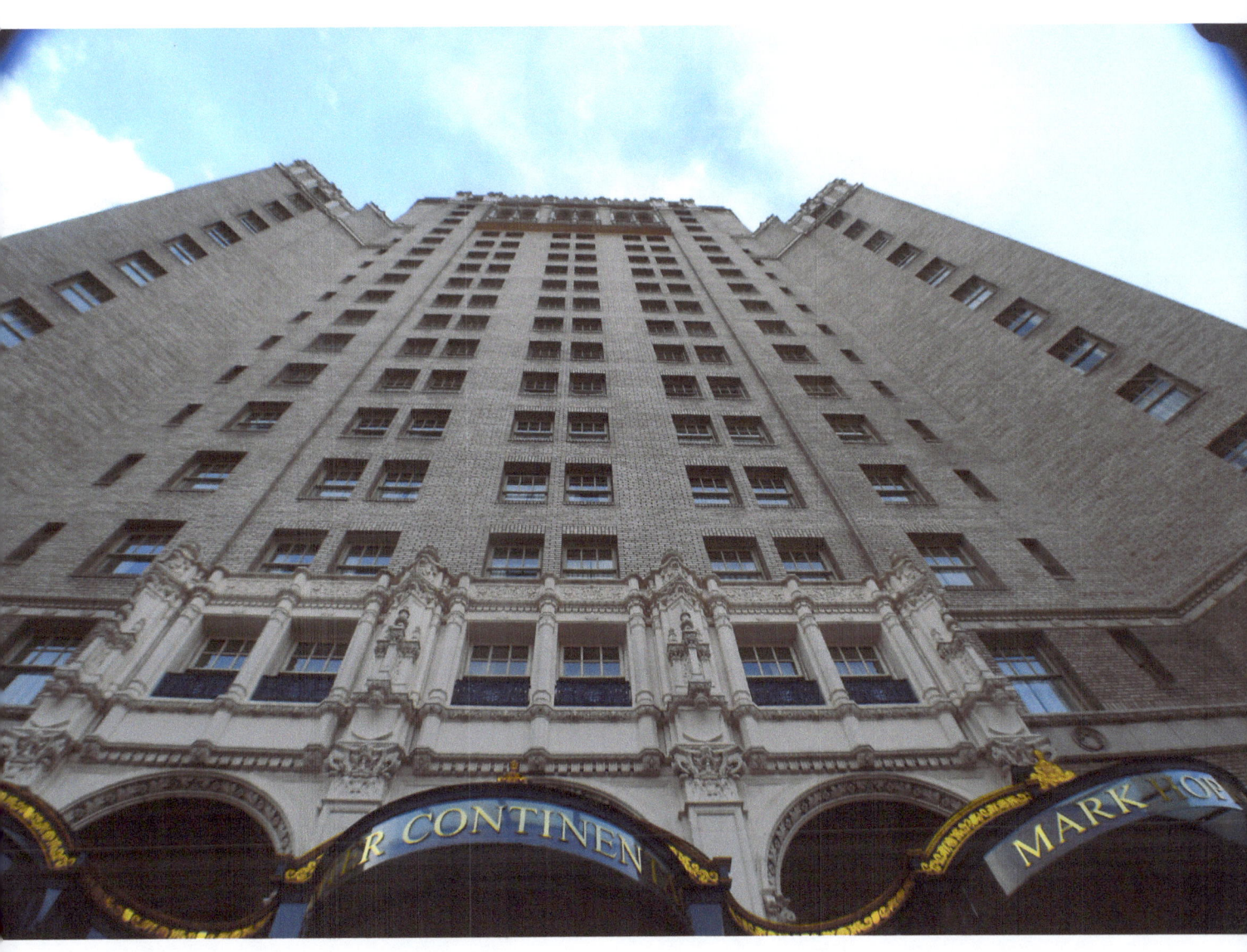

MARK HOPKINS HOTEL

The architectural firm Weeks and Day combined the styles of Spanish Ornamentation and French Chateau when they designed the Mark Hopkins Hotel. At 305 feet (92.97 meters) the Mark Hopkins has 20 floors containing 380 rooms, 39 suites and the famous glass-walled "Top Of The Mark" restaurant, which is located on the 19th floor.

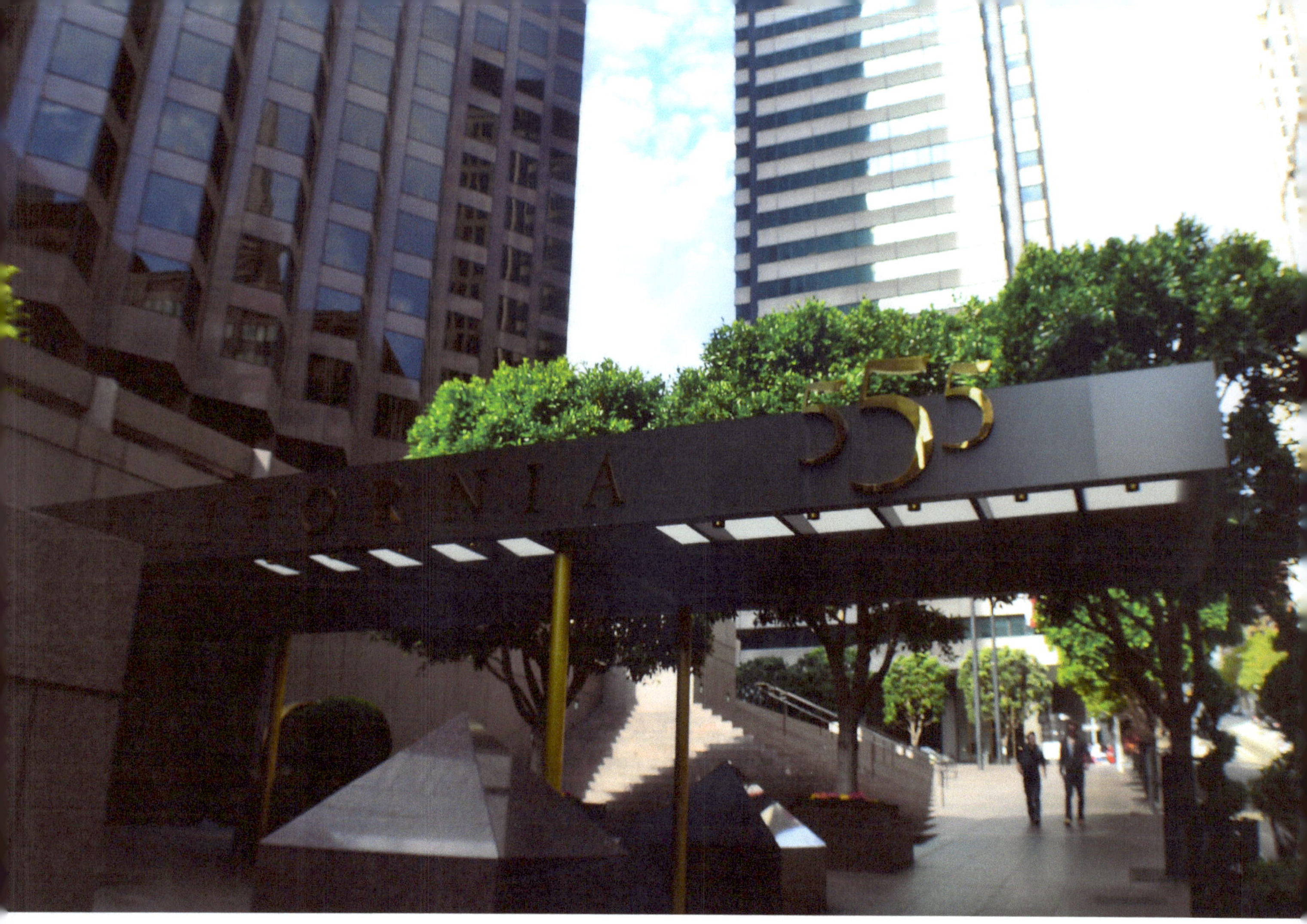
555

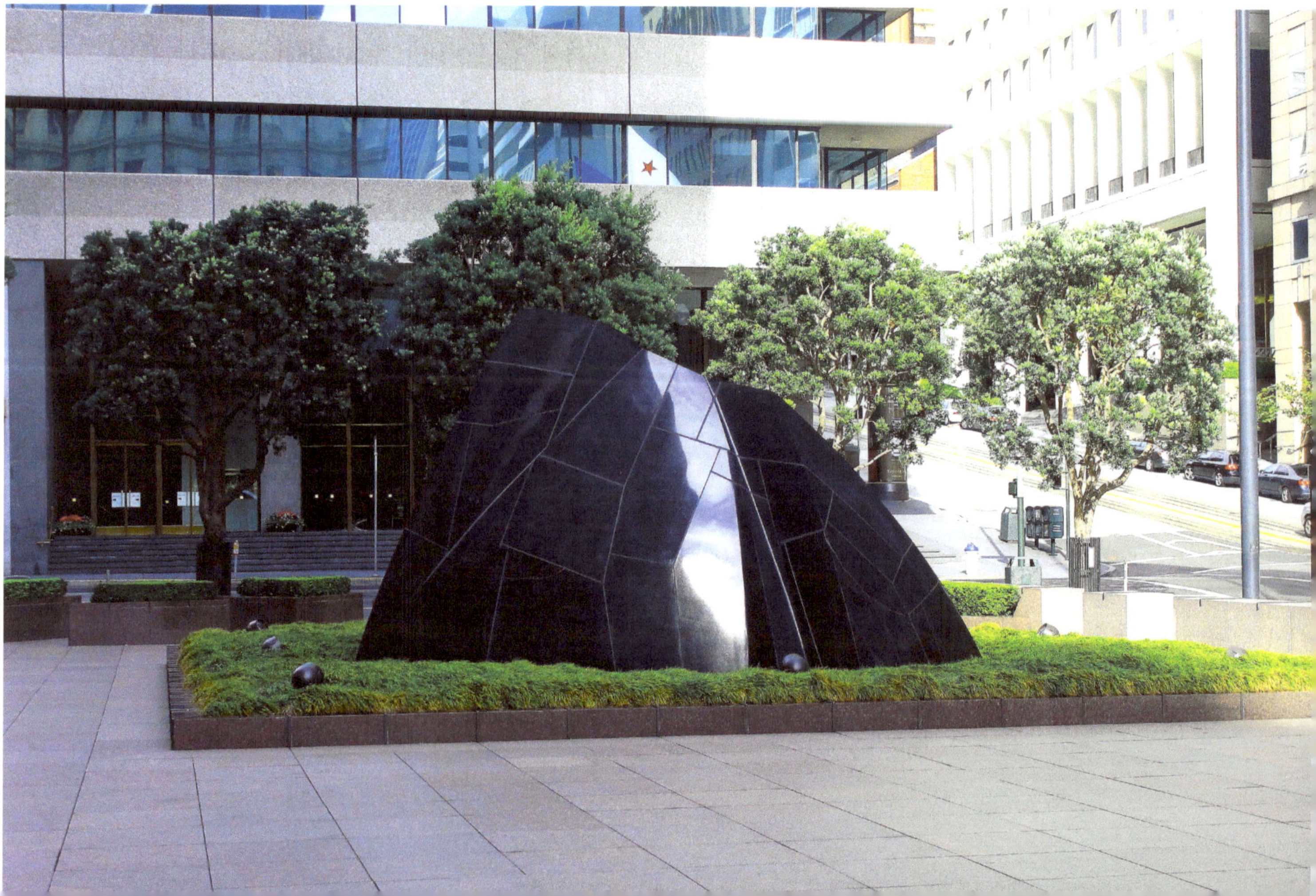

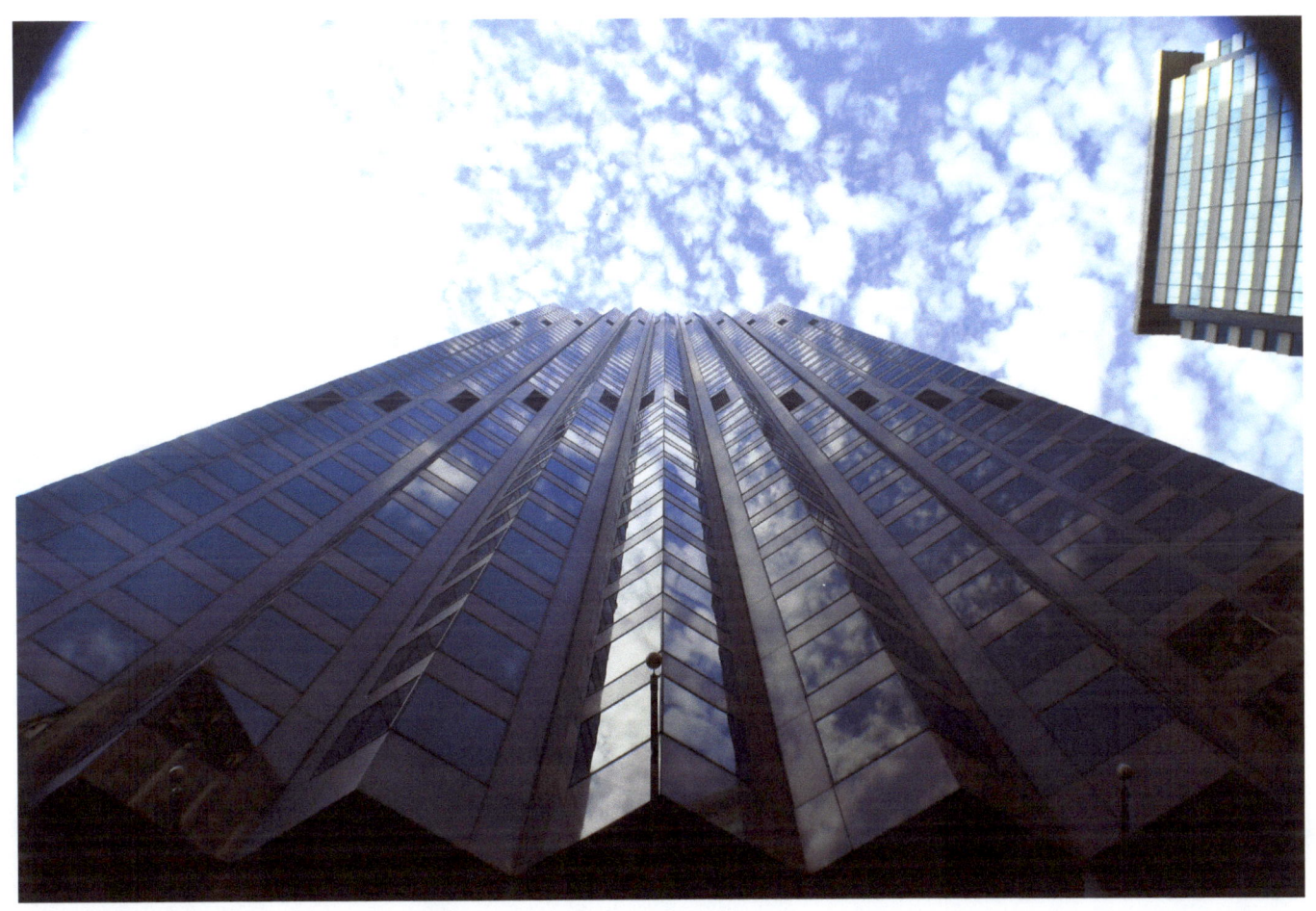

555 CALIFORNIA STREET

Two architecture firms- Wurster, Bernardi and Emmons and Skidmore, Owings and Merrill- along with one consulting architect, Pietro Belluschi, designed 555 California Street. Construction was completed in 1969. Standing at 779 feet (237.44 meters), 555 California Street contains 52 stories with a floor area of 1,800,000 square feet (167,225 square meters). The banking hall, stairways, sidewalks and the plaza are all clad in Carnelian Granite. Giannini Plaza contains a 200-ton sculpture named "Transcendence", known locally as "the banker's heart".[10]

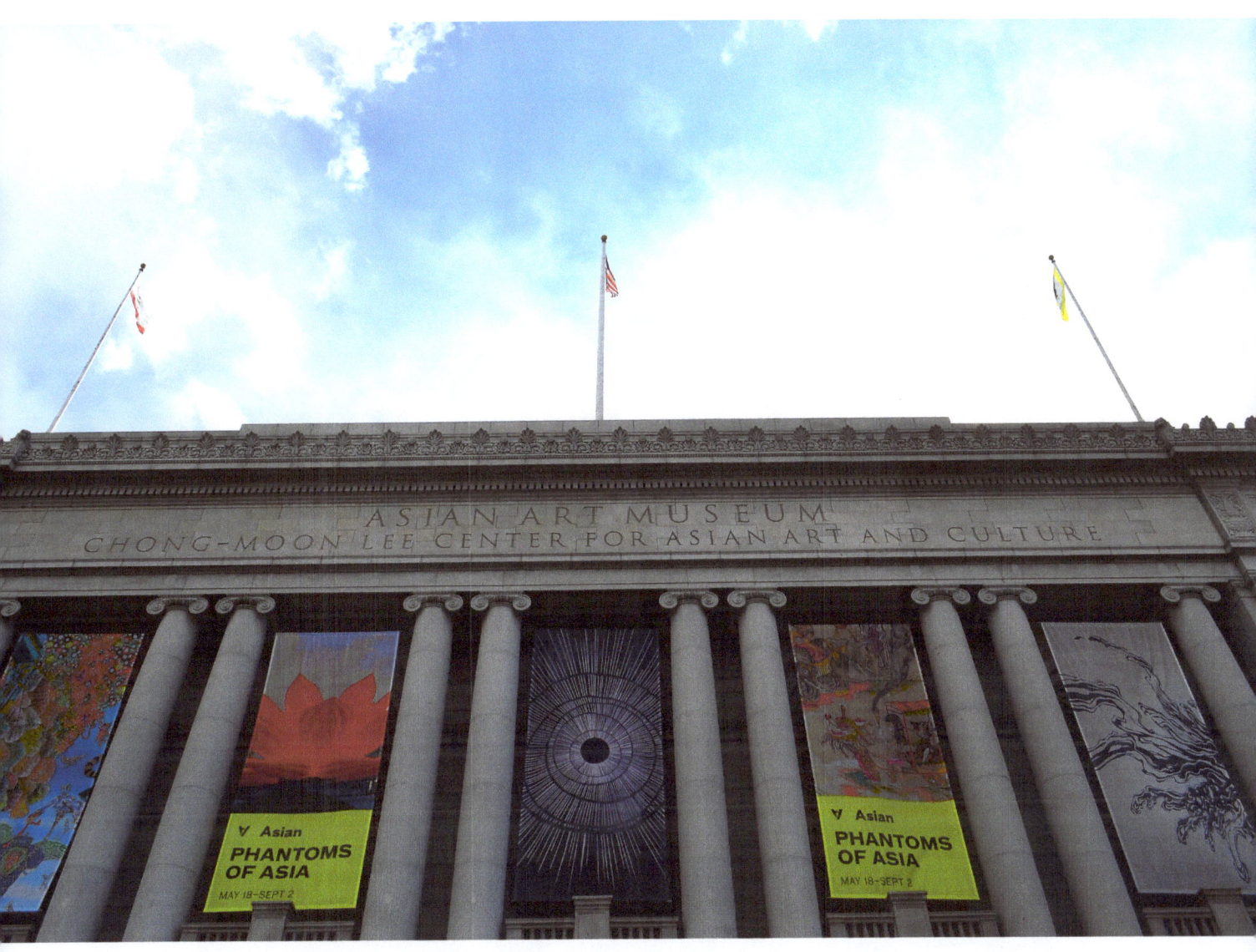

ASIAN ART MUSEUM

San Francisco's Asian Art Museum contains one of the largest collections of Asian art in the United States. The museum now occupies the old city library building, where it opened on March 20, 2003. The museum displays 17,000 works of Asian art and consists of 40,000 square feet of exhibit space.

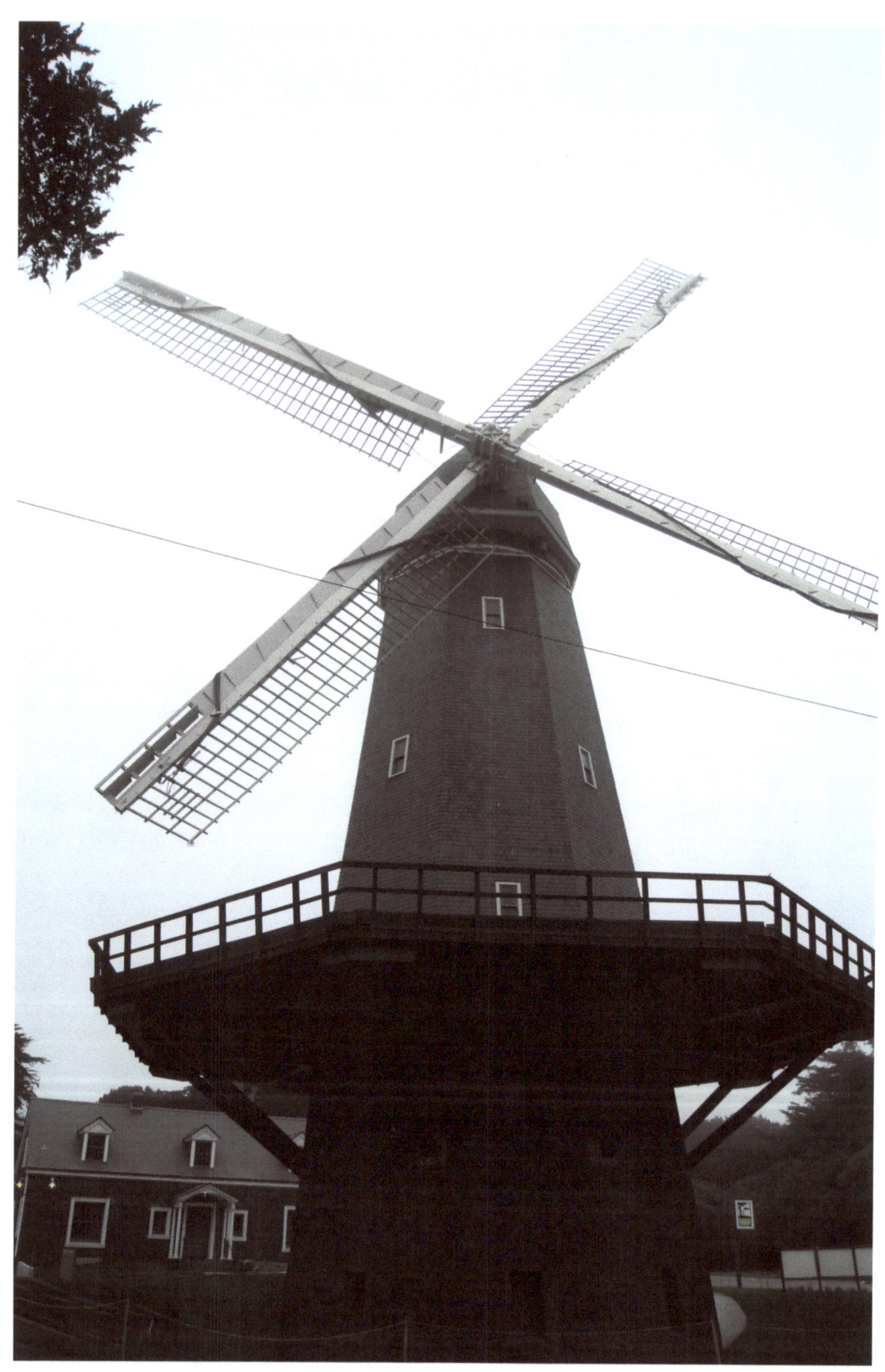

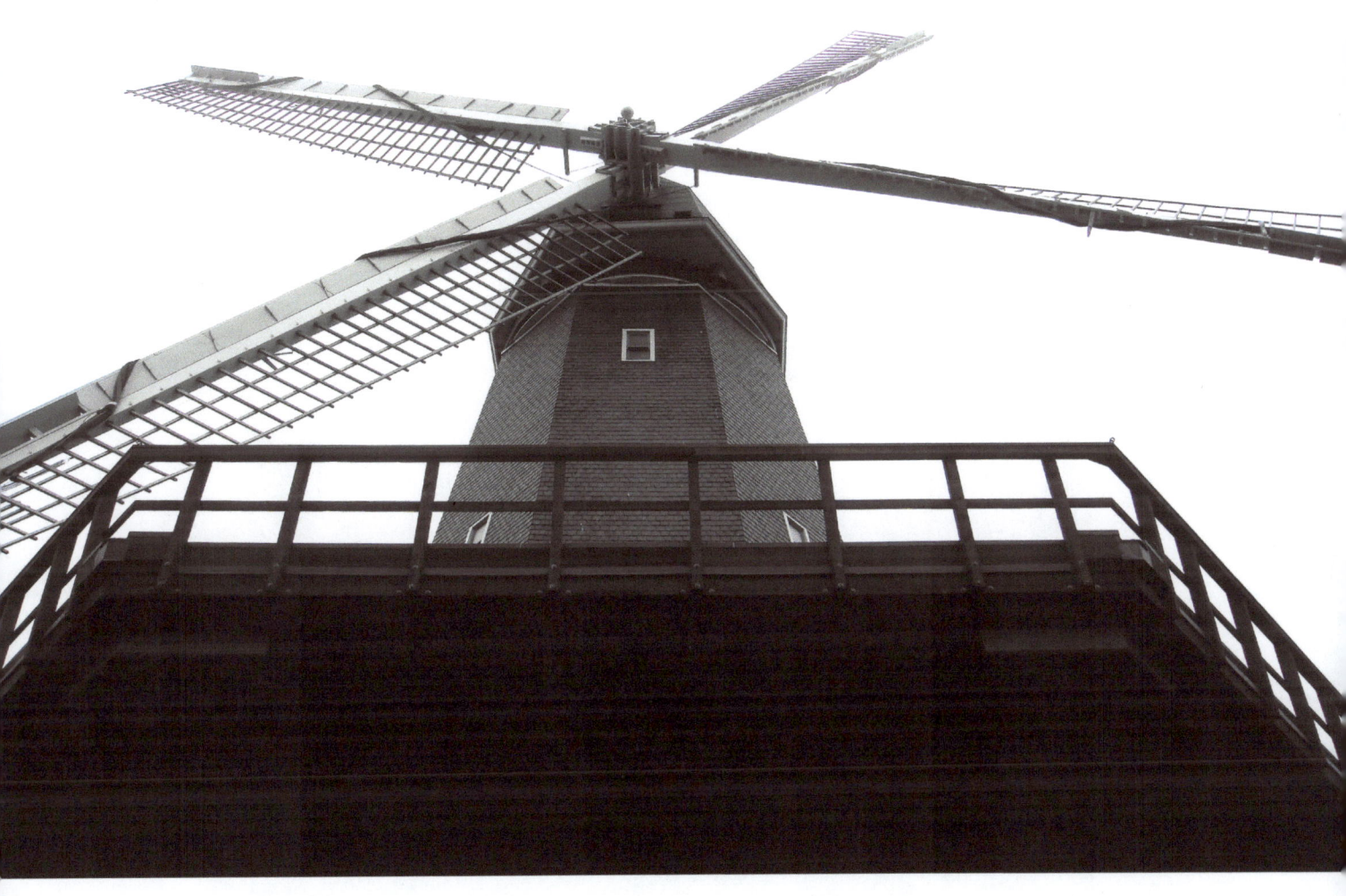

MURPHY WINDMILL

Golden Gate Park contains two windmills, one of which is Murphy Windmill, pictured here. Constructed in 1905, Murphy Windmill was originally used as a pumping station that supplied water to Stow Lake. In order to support the war effort, both windmills were stripped of their metal parts after the commencement of World War II. In 2001 a restoration project began, and continued through 2011. Murphy Windmill, now restored to it's former glory, contains sails that are 150 feet (45.72 meters) in diameter.

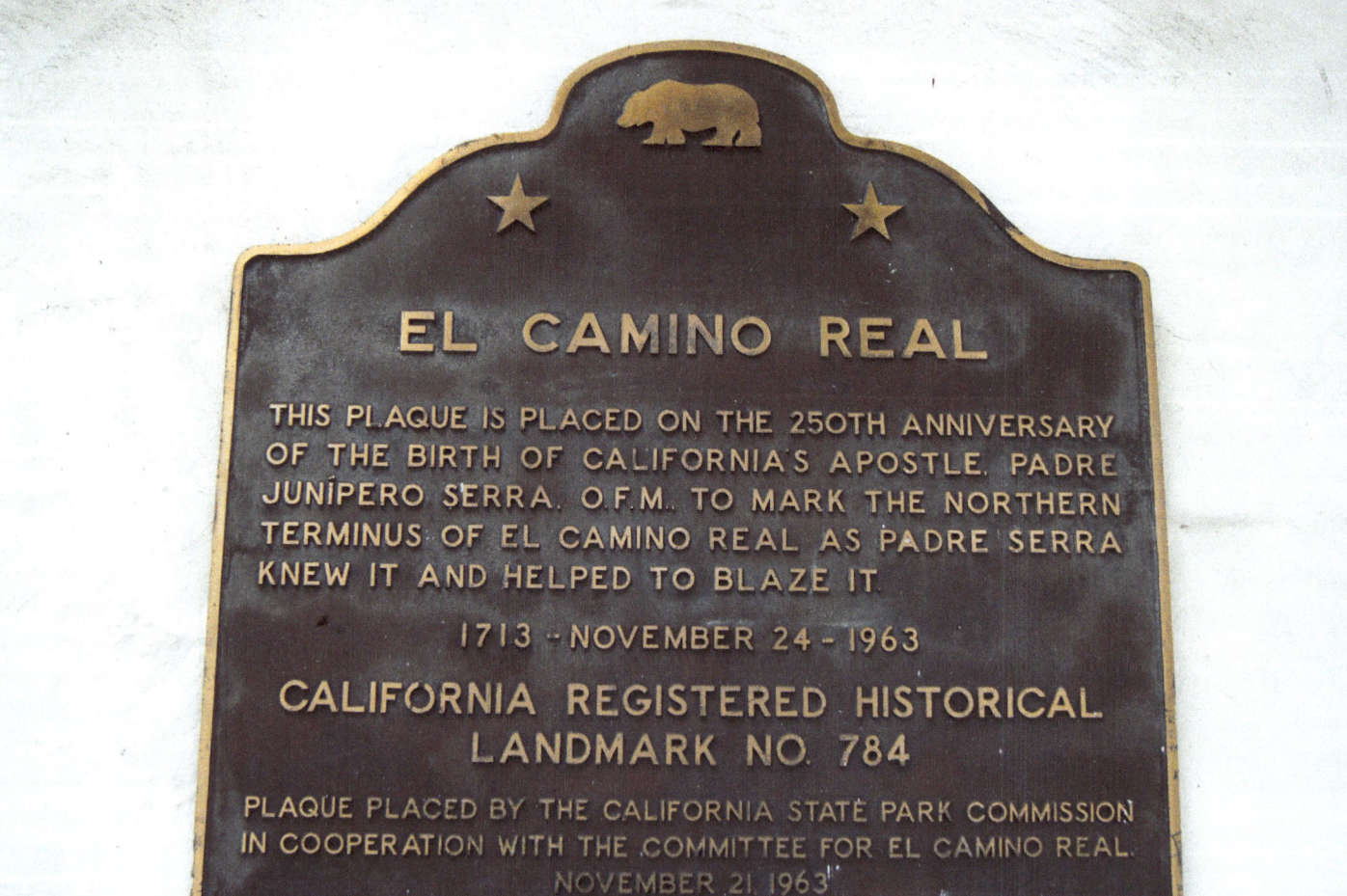

EL CAMINO REAL

THIS PLAQUE IS PLACED ON THE 250TH ANNIVERSARY
OF THE BIRTH OF CALIFORNIA'S APOSTLE, PADRE
JUNIPERO SERRA, O.F.M., TO MARK THE NORTHERN
TERMINUS OF EL CAMINO REAL AS PADRE SERRA
KNEW IT AND HELPED TO BLAZE IT.

1713 - NOVEMBER 24 - 1963

CALIFORNIA REGISTERED HISTORICAL
LANDMARK NO. 784

PLAQUE PLACED BY THE CALIFORNIA STATE PARK COMMISSION
IN COOPERATION WITH THE COMMITTEE FOR EL CAMINO REAL.
NOVEMBER 21, 1963

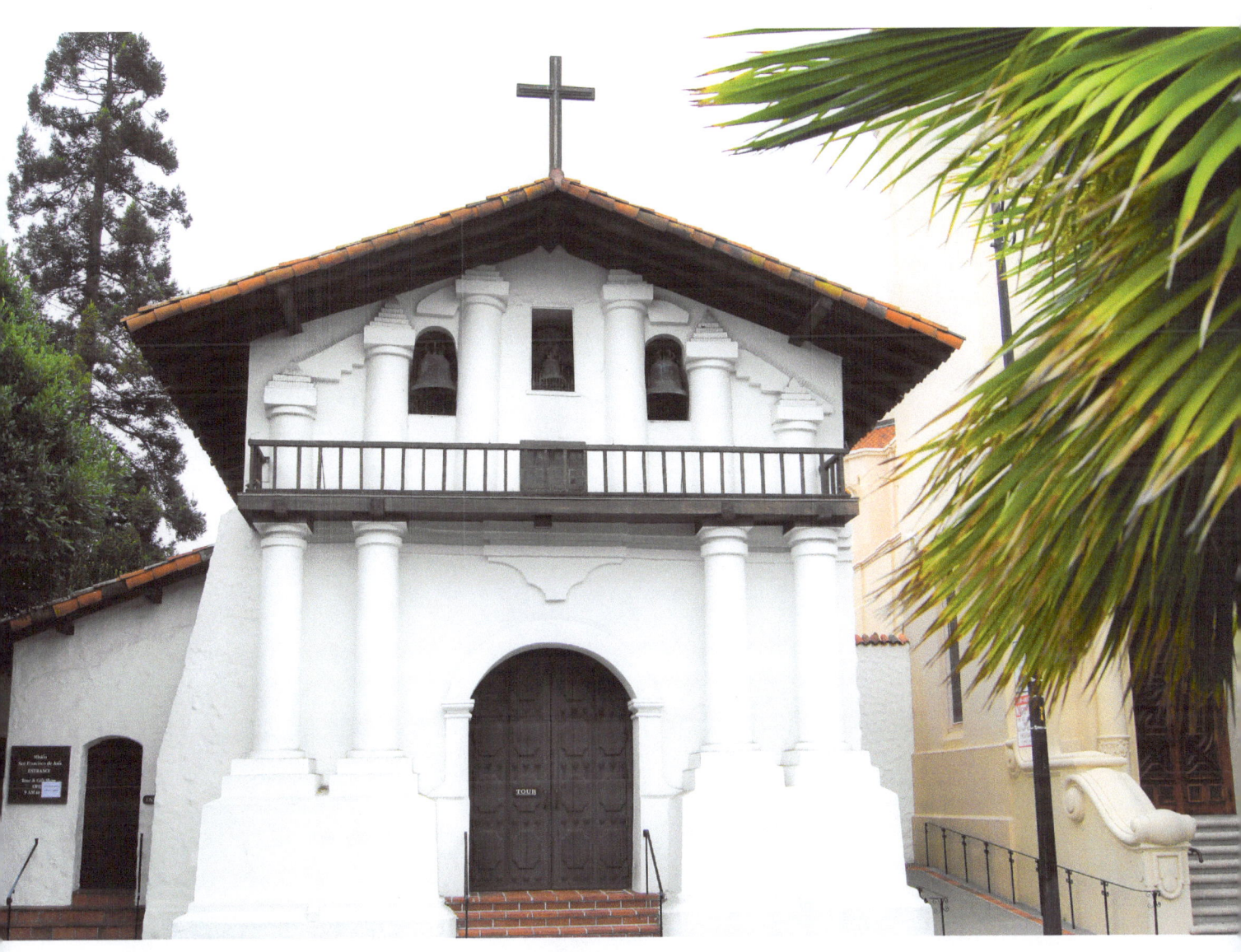

MISSION DOLORES

Mission Dolores is the oldest building in San Francisco. Founded the 29th of June 1776 by Padre Junipero Serra, the Mission has survived multiple earthquakes (the 1906 quake as well as the 1989 quake) and has remained a solid symbol of faith in its community.

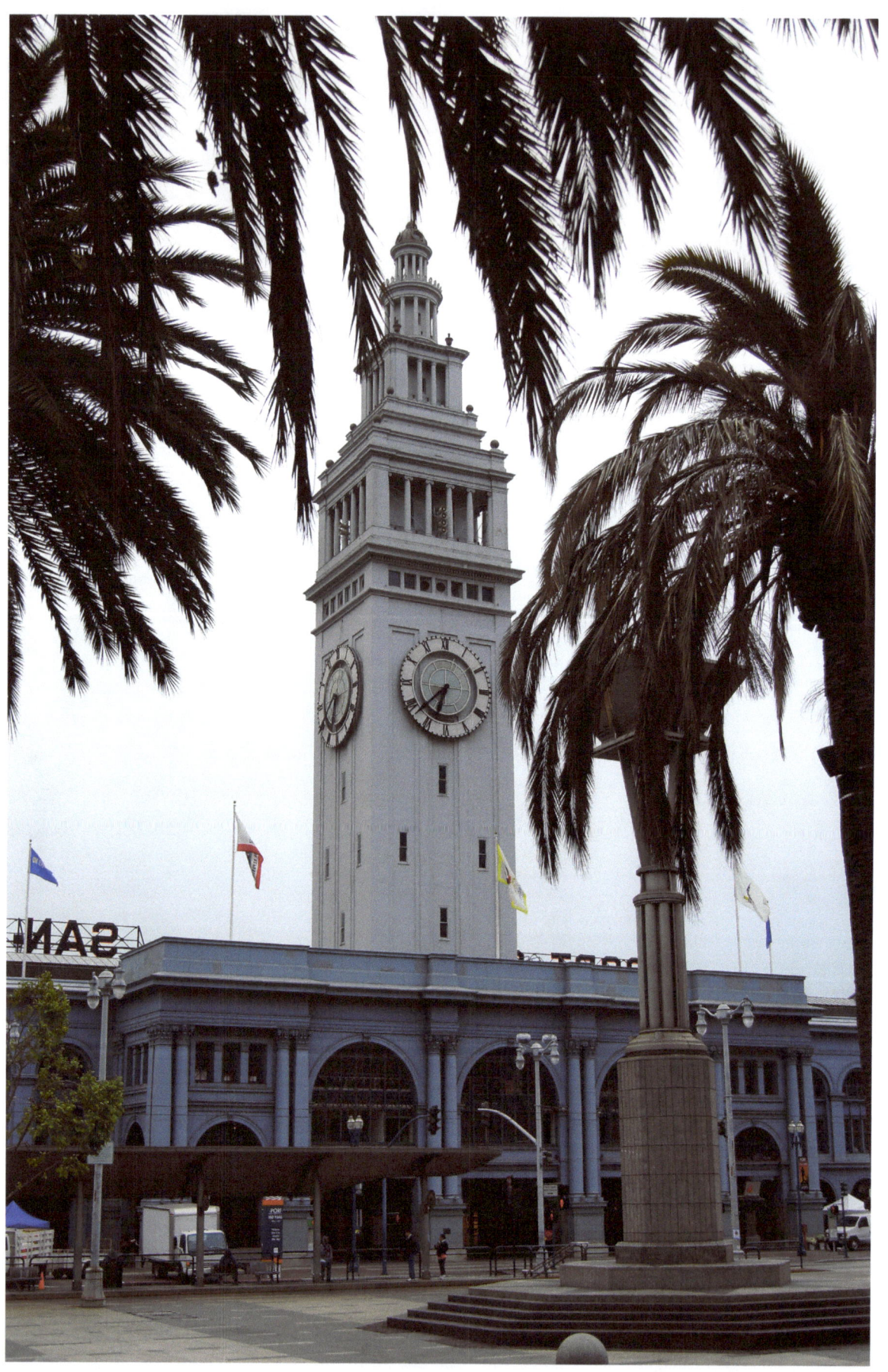

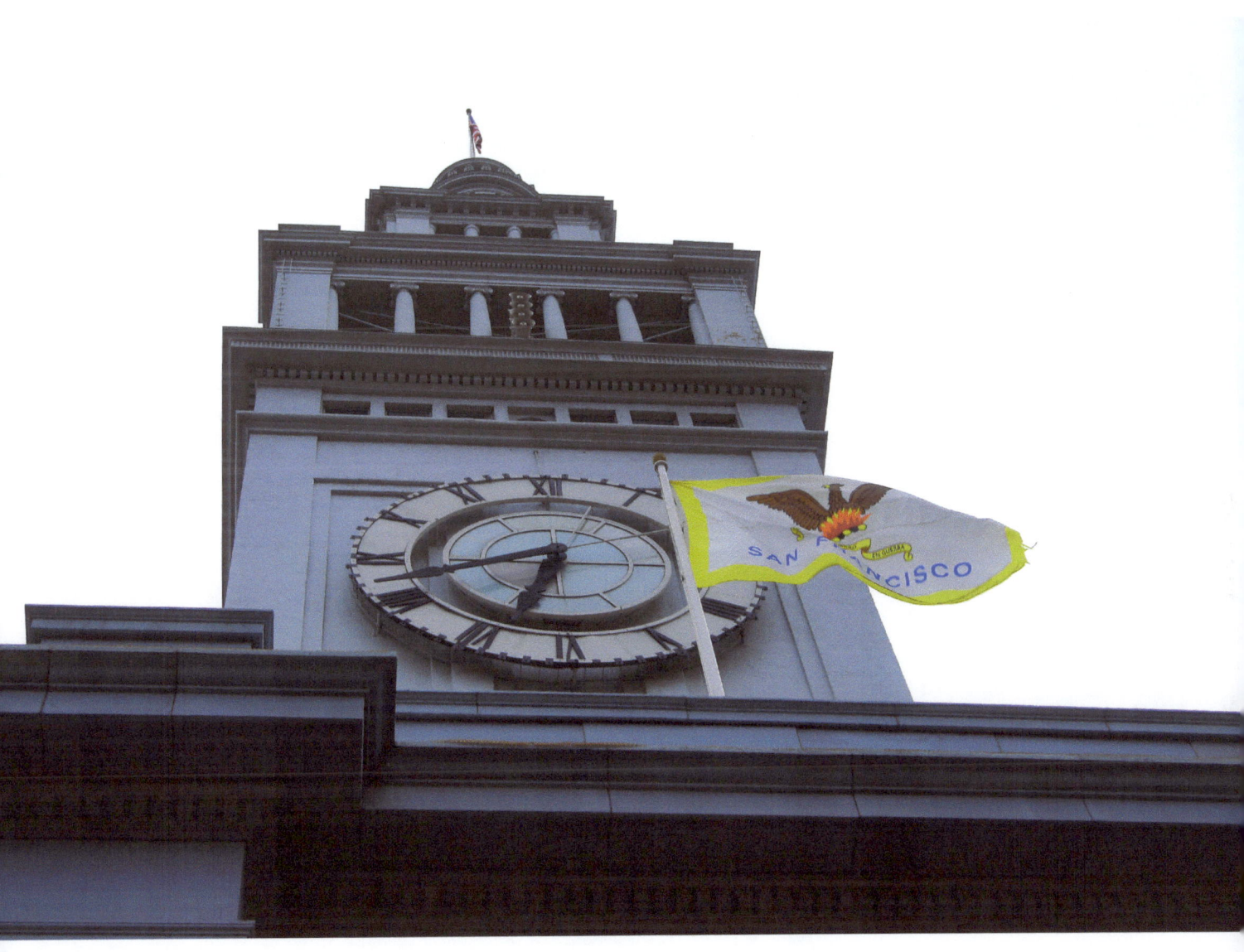

FERRY BUILDING

The San Francisco Ferry Building was designed by Arthur Page Brown in 1892 and was opened for business in 1898. Rising above the building is a clock tower measuring 245 feet (74.68 meters), which contains the world's largest dialed, wind-up, mechanical clock. The complex also contains docking platforms for multiple ferries, as well as shops and cafés.

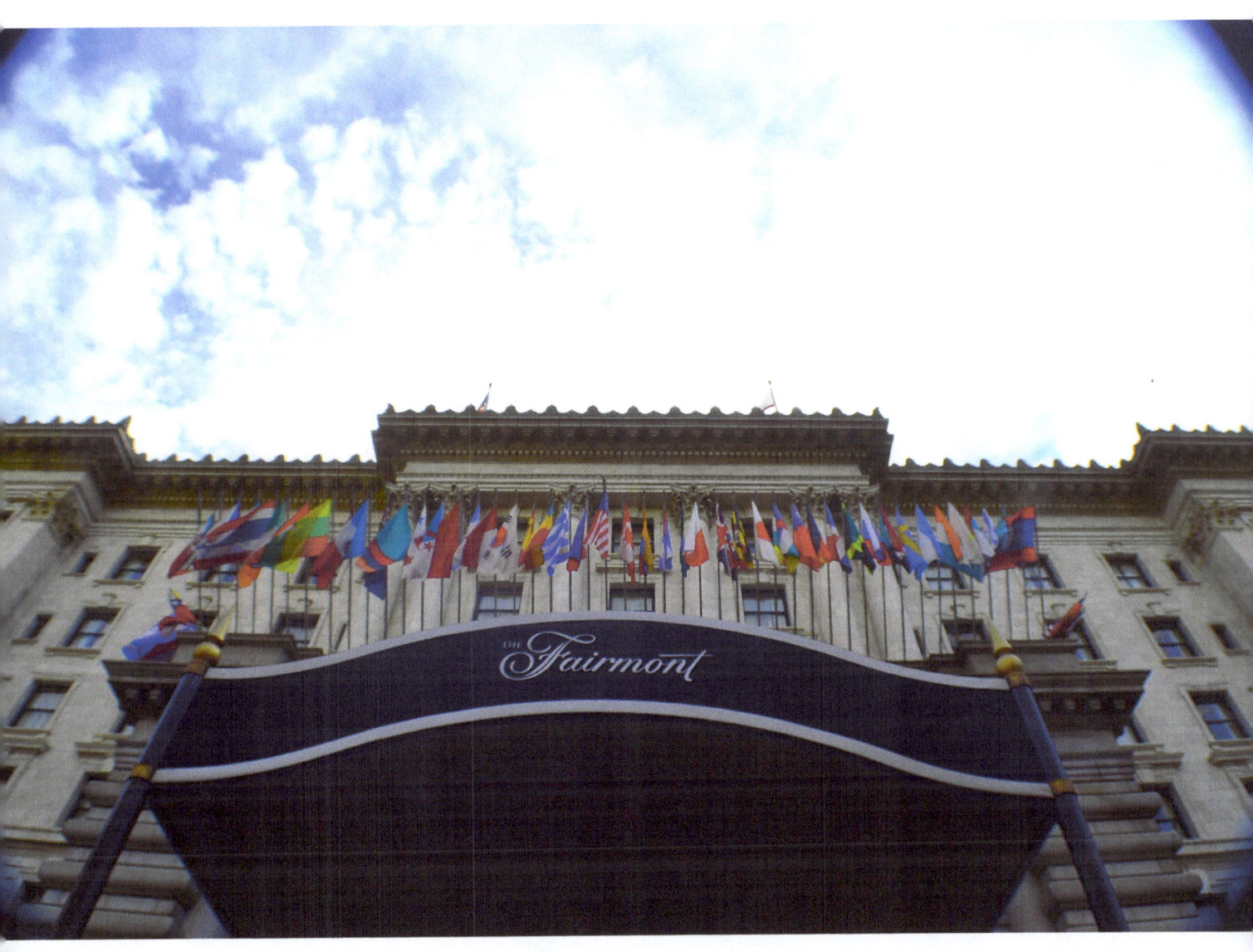

THE FAIRMONT HOTEL

Because of the 1906 earthquake, the Fairmont Hotel did not open as scheduled, it's opening date was delayed until 1907. Designed by architects Reid and Reid, Ira Wilson Hoover, and Julia Morgan; the Fairmont hotel comprises two separate structures-- the main hotel and a tower that was added in 1962. The Fairmont contains 591 rooms, and three restaurants, the Tonga Room and Hurricane Bar, Caffe Cento, and the Laurel Court Restaurant and Bar. The main hotel rises 90 feet (27.43 meters) and consists of nine floors, while the tower, which stands at 325 feet (99.06 meters), contains 29.

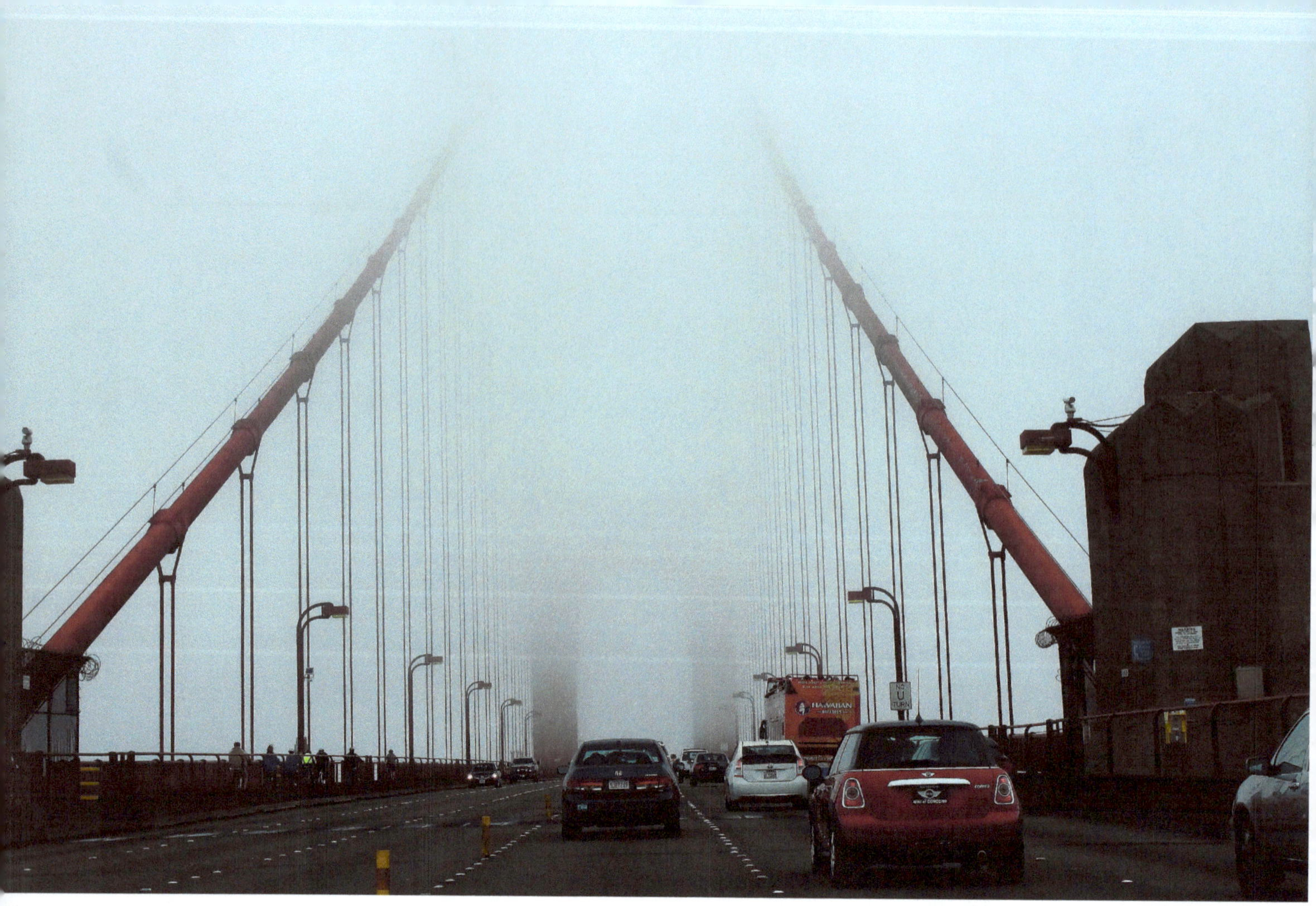
NO
U
TURN

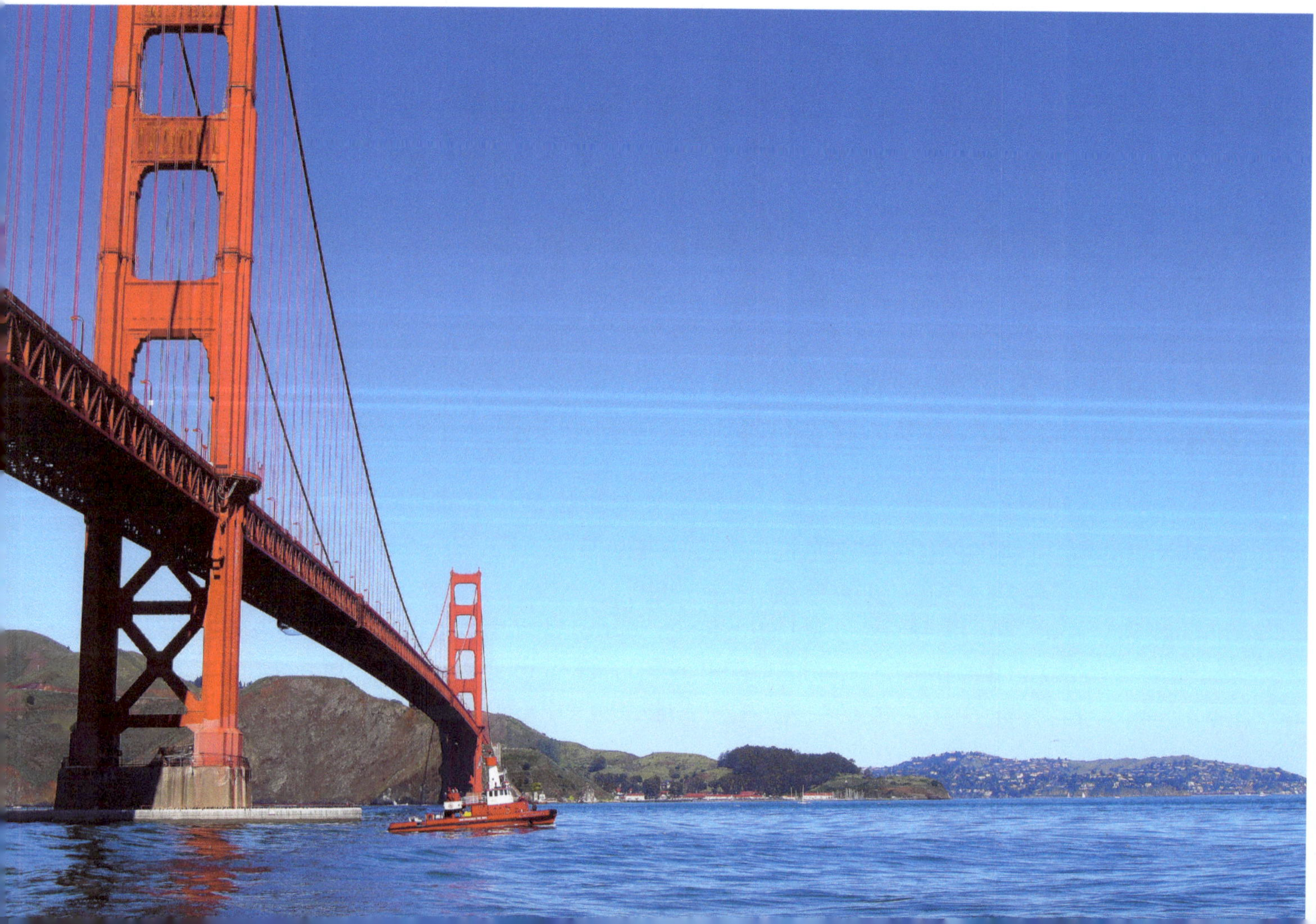

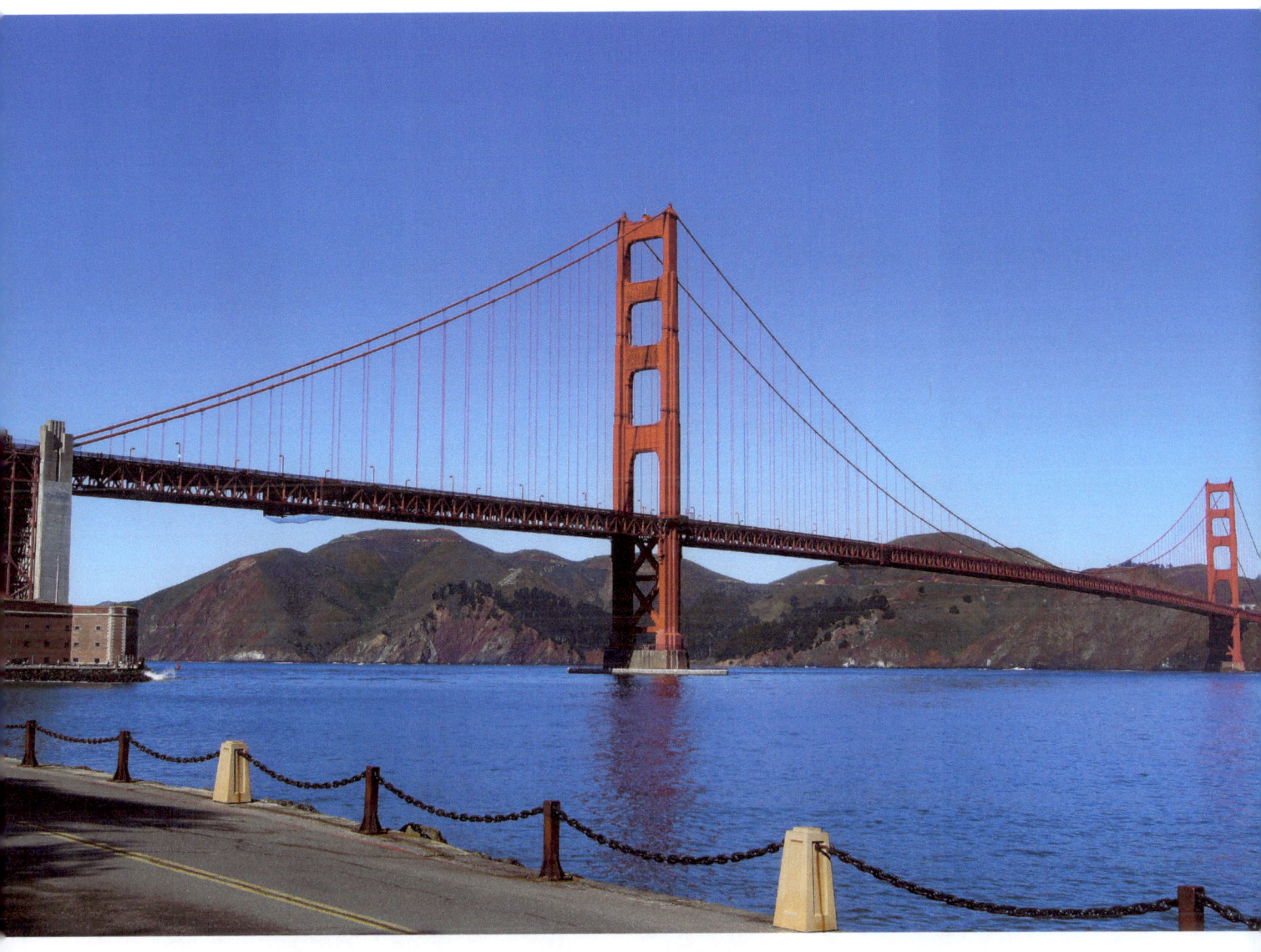

THE GOLDEN GATE BRIDGE

The Golden Gate Bridge is a suspension bridge that stretches from San Francisco to the Marin County headlands. The bridge's construction began on January 5, 1933, and ended on April 19th 1937; it officially opened on May 27, 1937. The bridge was designed by many architects and engineers notably; Joseph Strauss, Irving Morrow as a consulting architect, and Charles Ellis.

The Golden Gate Bridge stretches 1.7 miles (2.7 kilometers), the longest span being 4,200 feet (1,280 meters). With a width of 90 feet (27 meters) the bridge holds 6 lanes of traffic, that suspend 220 feet above the water (67 meters, at tide). With its two towers standing at an incredible 746 feet (227 meters), and its total length stretching almost two miles the Golden Gate Bridge has earned its place as one of the Seven Wonders of the Modern World.

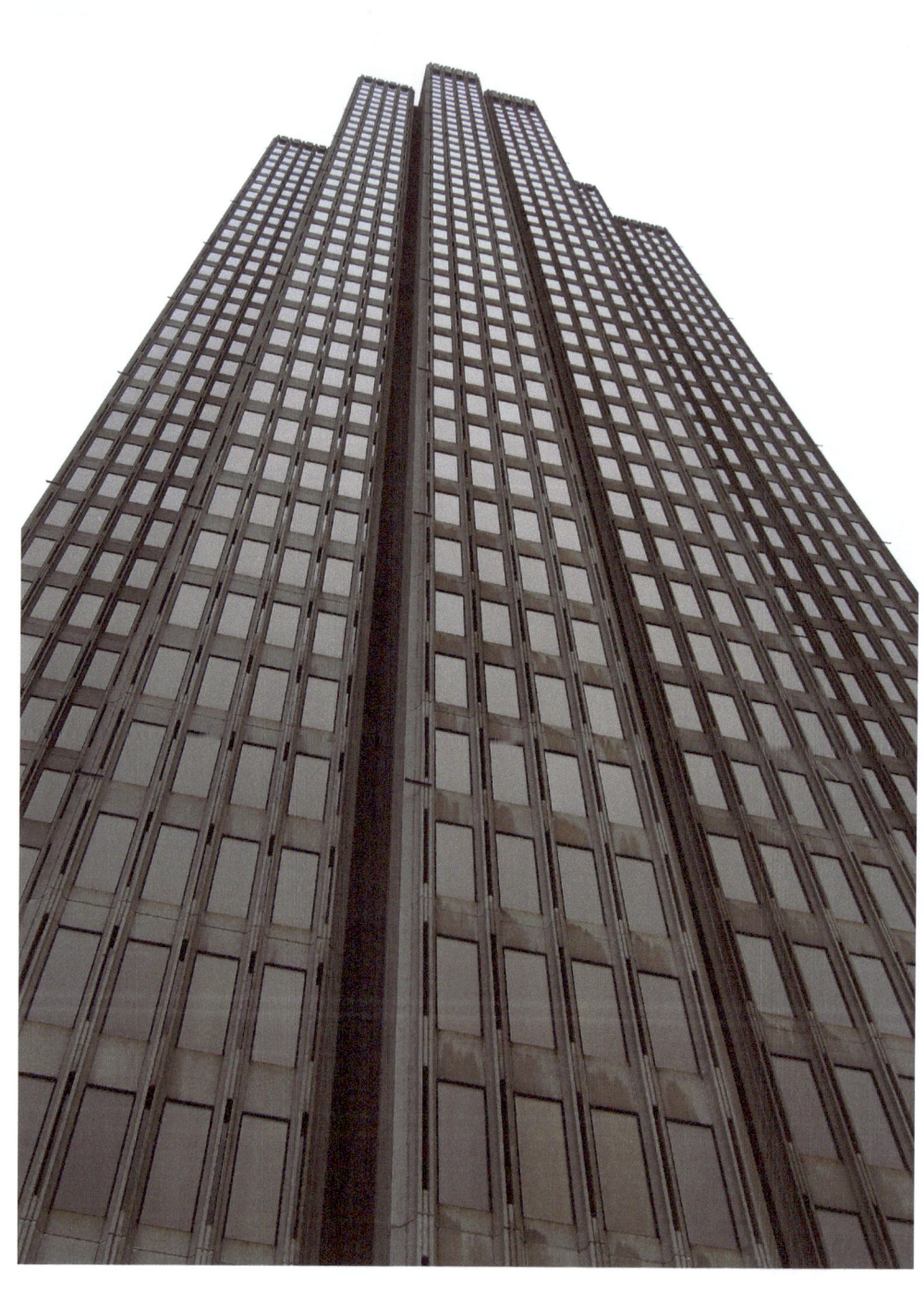

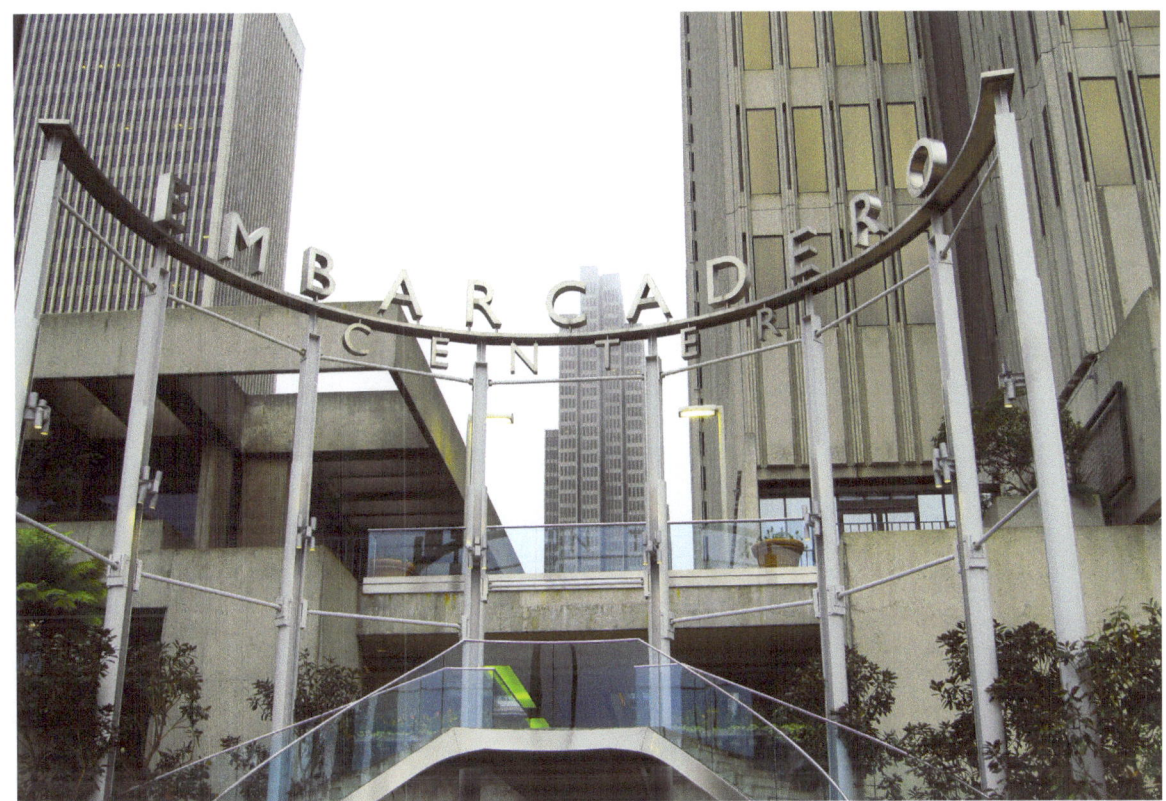

EMBARCADERO CENTER

Embarcadero Center is a large commercial complex that was developed by Trammell-Crow, John Portman and David Rockefeller. Embarcadero Center consists of 7 buildings and covers 8.5 acres (3.4 hectares). Four of the seven buildings were constructed in the 1970's.

Completed in 1971, One Embarcadero contains 45 floors and rises to a height of 569 feet (173.43 meters). Five Embarcadero, (also known as the Hyatt Regency Hotel) was completed in 1973. Five Embarcadero rises to a height of 252 feet (76.80 meters) and contains 20 floors. Completed in 1974, Two Embarcadero contains 30 floors and has a height of 413 feet (125.88 meters). Three Embarcadero was the last of the buildings to be constructed in the 1970's. Completed in 1977, Three Embarcadero contains 31 floors and rises 413 feet (125.88 meters).

The three remaining buildings were constructed in the 1980's. Completed in 1982, Four Embarcadero is the tallest building in the complex. Four Embarcadero contains 45 floors and rises to a height of 570 feet (173.73 meters). The sixth building to be completed was constructed in 1988. The hotel Le Meridien San Francisco rises to a height of 316 feet (96.31 meters) and contains 25 floors. The seventh and final building to be constructed was Embarcadero West. Completed in 1989, Embarcadero West contains 34 floors and rises to a height of 403 feet (122.83 meters).

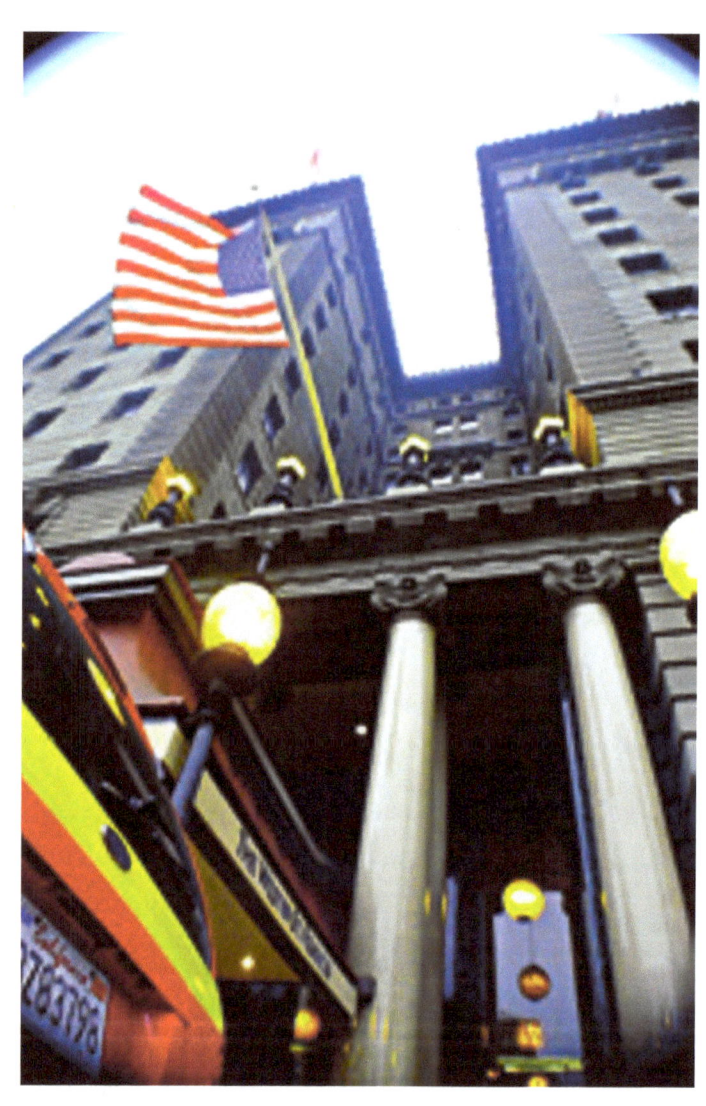

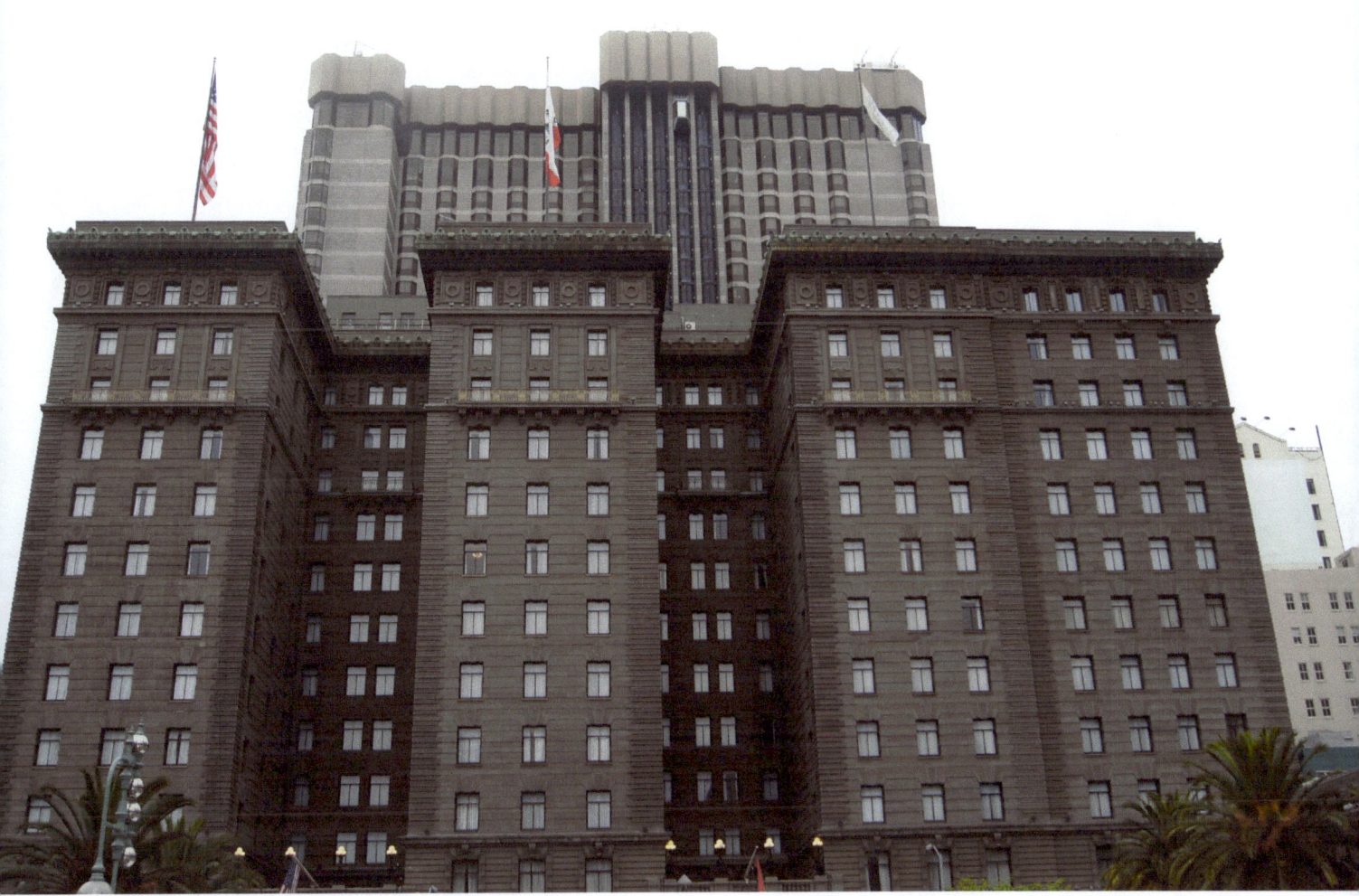

THE ST. FRANCIS HOTEL

The St. Francis Hotel was designed by architects Bliss and Faville along with the firm William L. Pereira and Associates. Opened in 1904, the St. Francis contains 12 floors, 616 rooms, and stands at 198 feet (60.35 meters). An additional tower containing 5 glass elevators that provide breathtaking views of the city and Union Square was added in 1972. Rising 393 feet (120 meters), the tower contains 581 rooms, and 32 floors. The St. Francis is one of the most well-known hotels in the city.

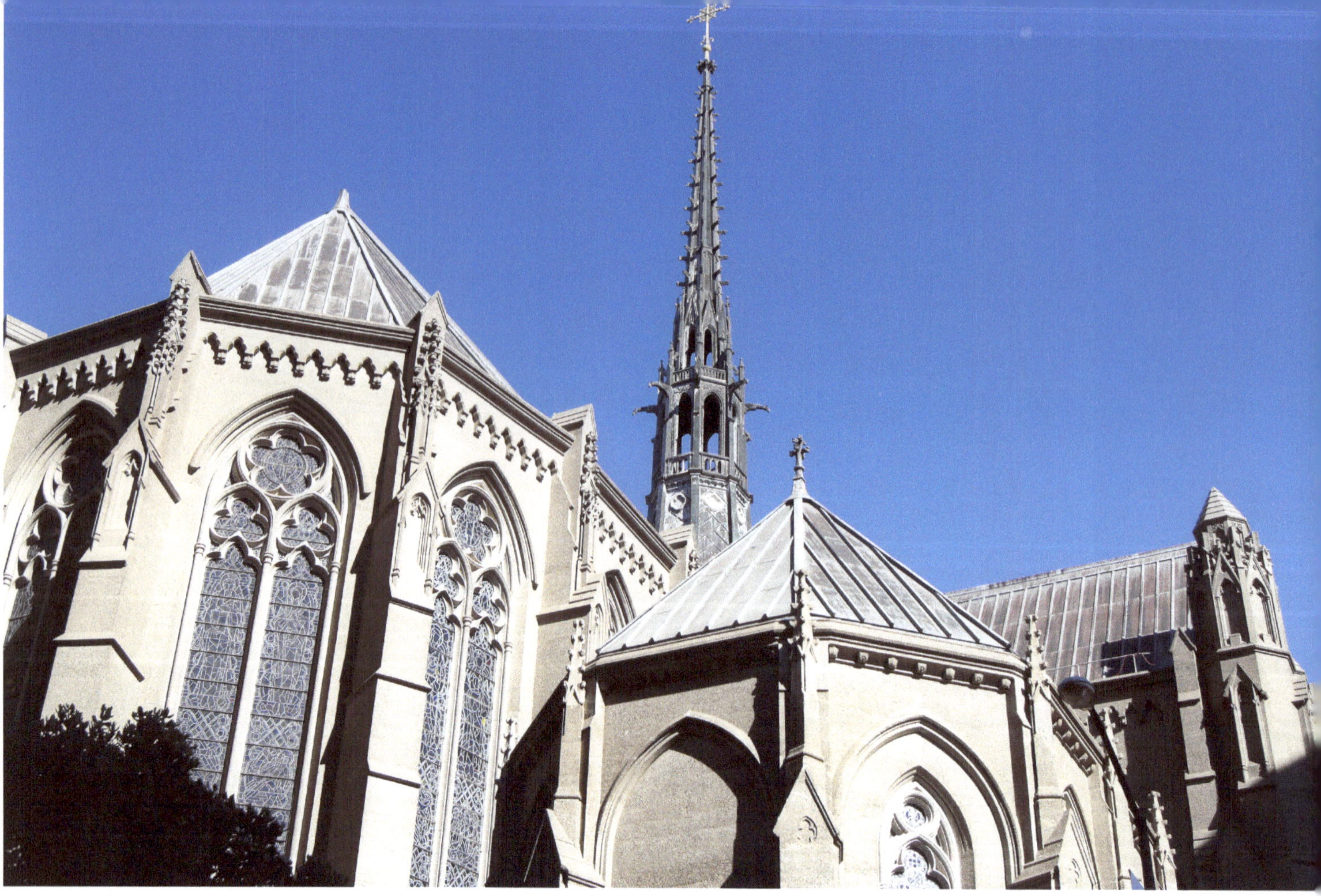

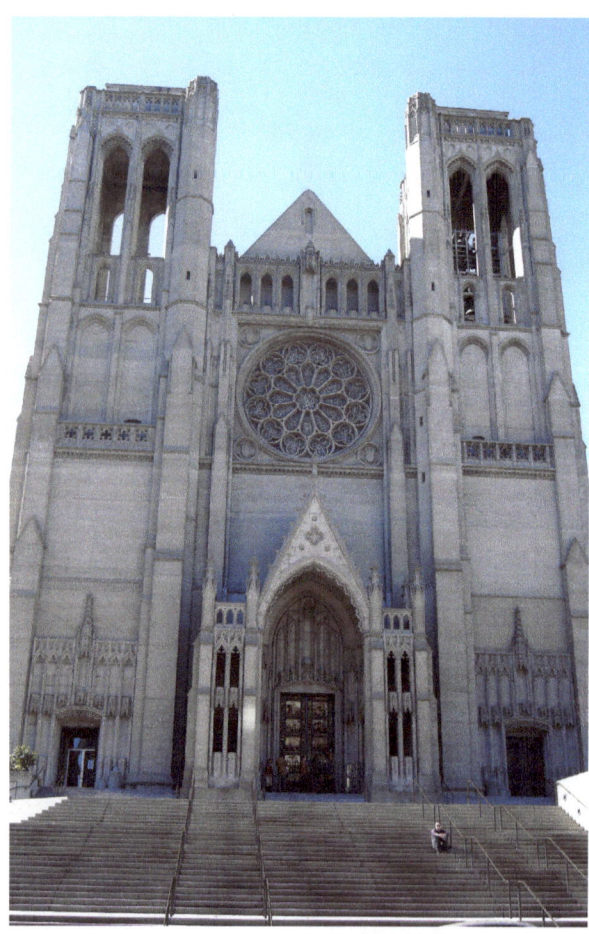

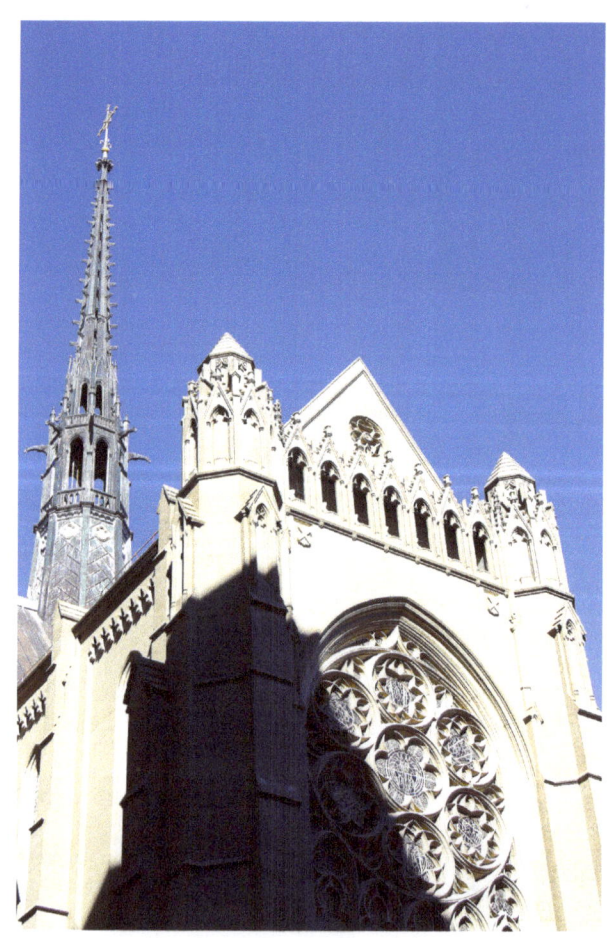

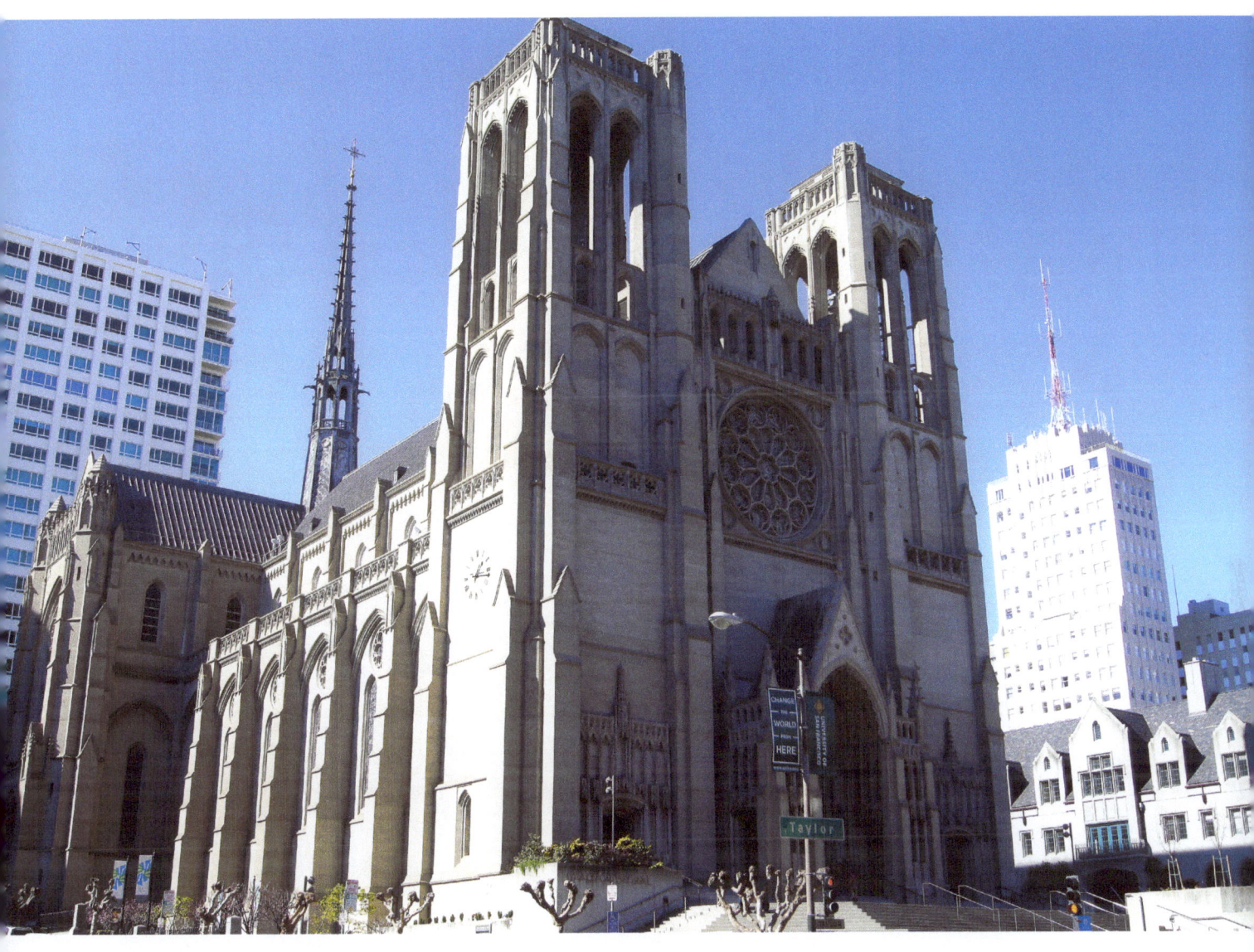

GRACE CATHEDRAL

Grace Church was originally founded in 1849; tragically, the church was destroyed during the 1906 earthquake. Lewis P. Hobart designed the current cathedral in a French Gothic style. Construction began in 1927 and was completed in 1964. Grace Cathedral contains many features, some of which include; a 44- bell Carillon, two labyrinths, and 7,290 square feet (677.26 square meters) of stained glass. The towers of Grace Cathedral rise to a height of 174 feet (53.03 meters), while the cross mounted on top of her steeple towers above them at 247 feet (75.28 meters).

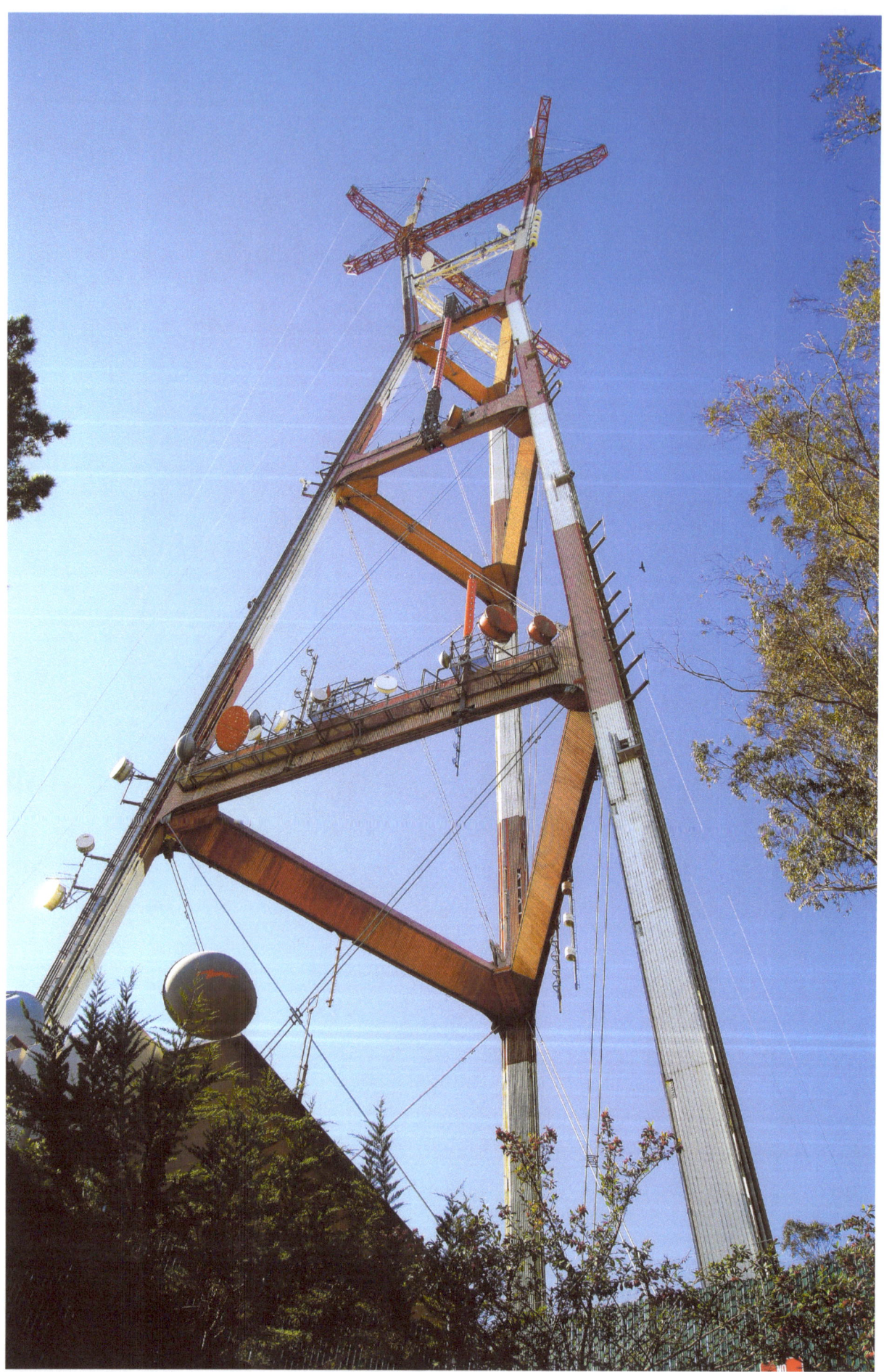

SUTRO TOWER

Sutro Tower is a radio antenna tower that broadcasts television and radio signals throughout the San Francisco Bay area. In 1971, to the complete dismay of many locals, Kline Towers began construction of what some have come to call the "Sutro Monster". Standing at 977 feet (298 meters) and weighing in at 3.5 million pounds (1,588 metric tons) Sutro Tower is one of the most iconic symbols of San Francisco. Final construction of the "Sutro Monster" occured in 1973.

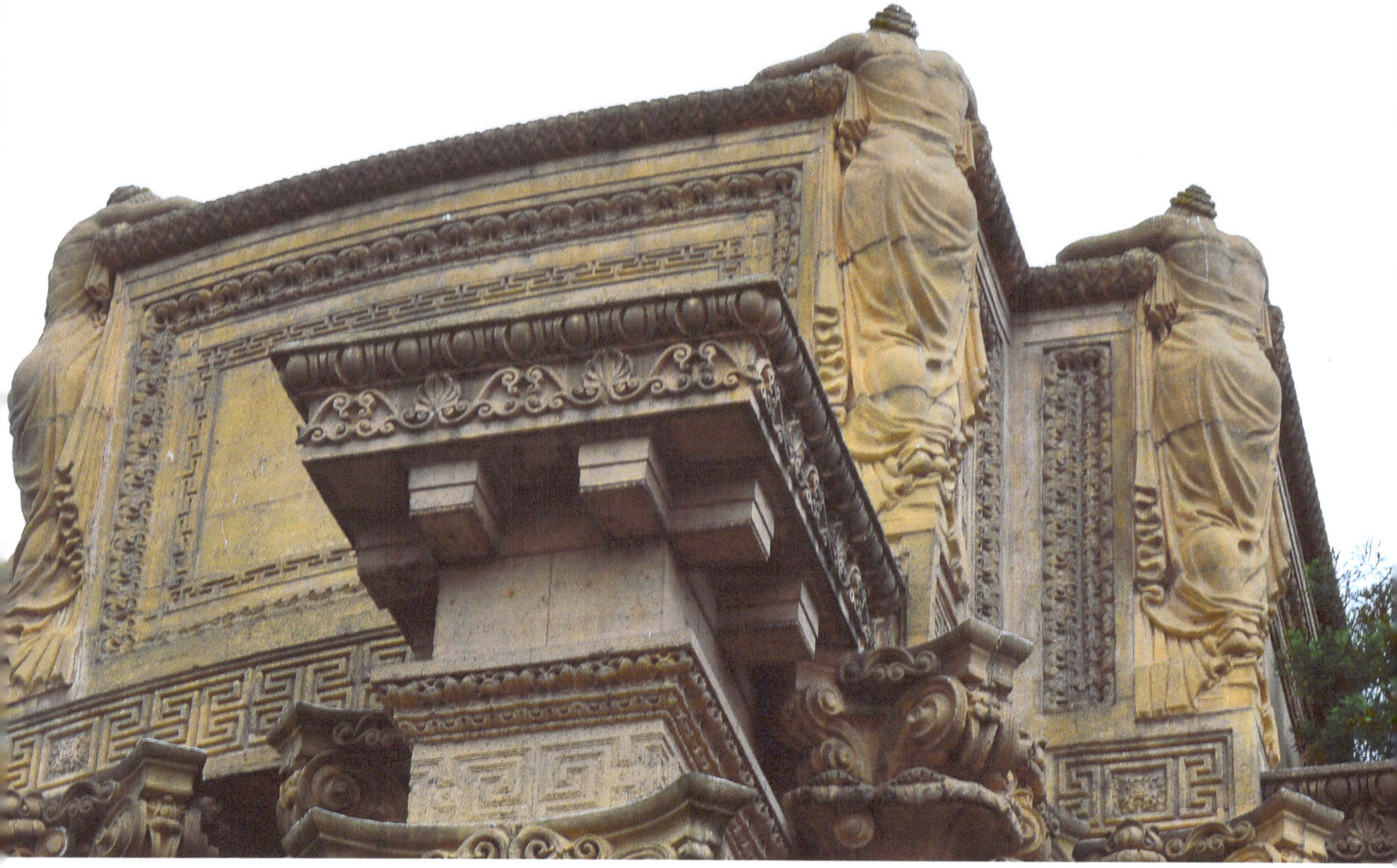

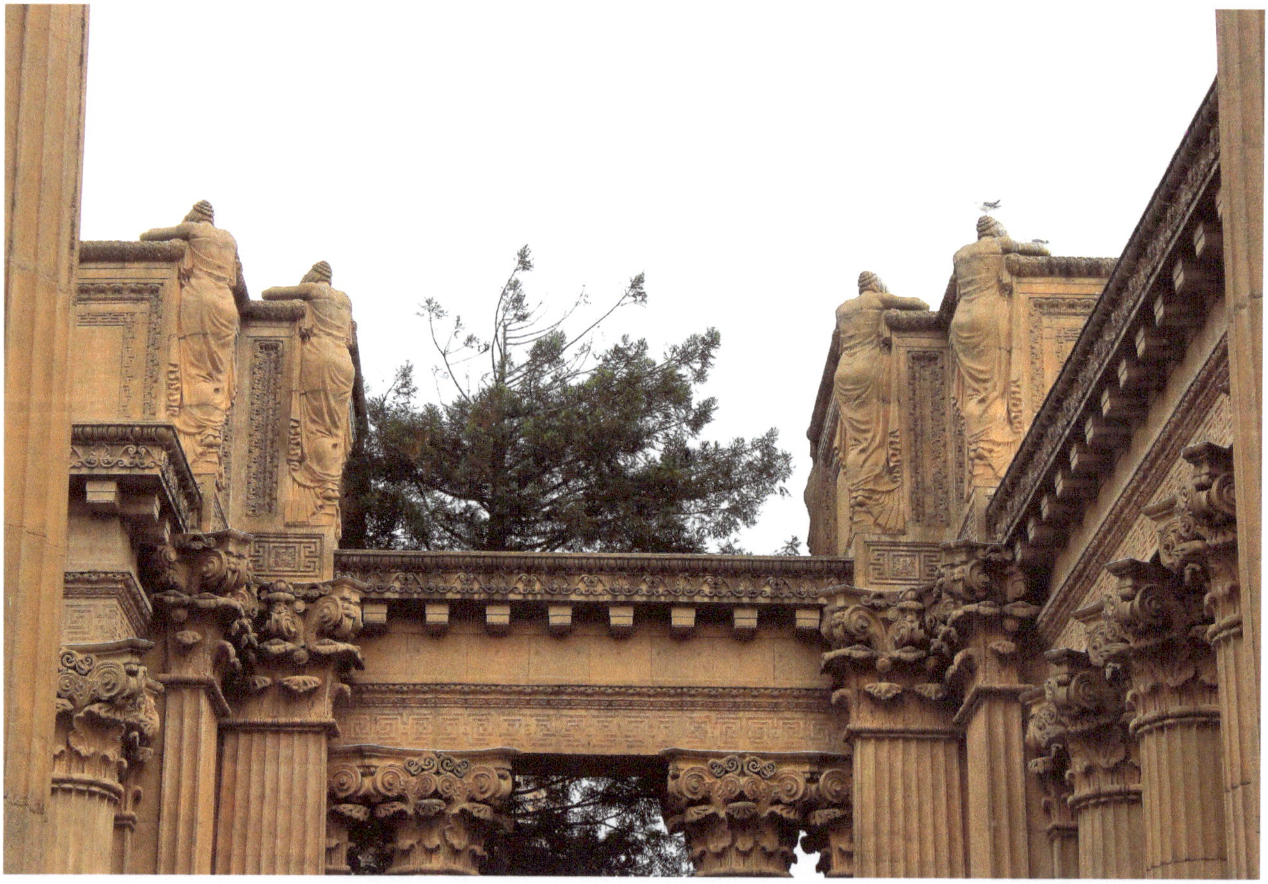

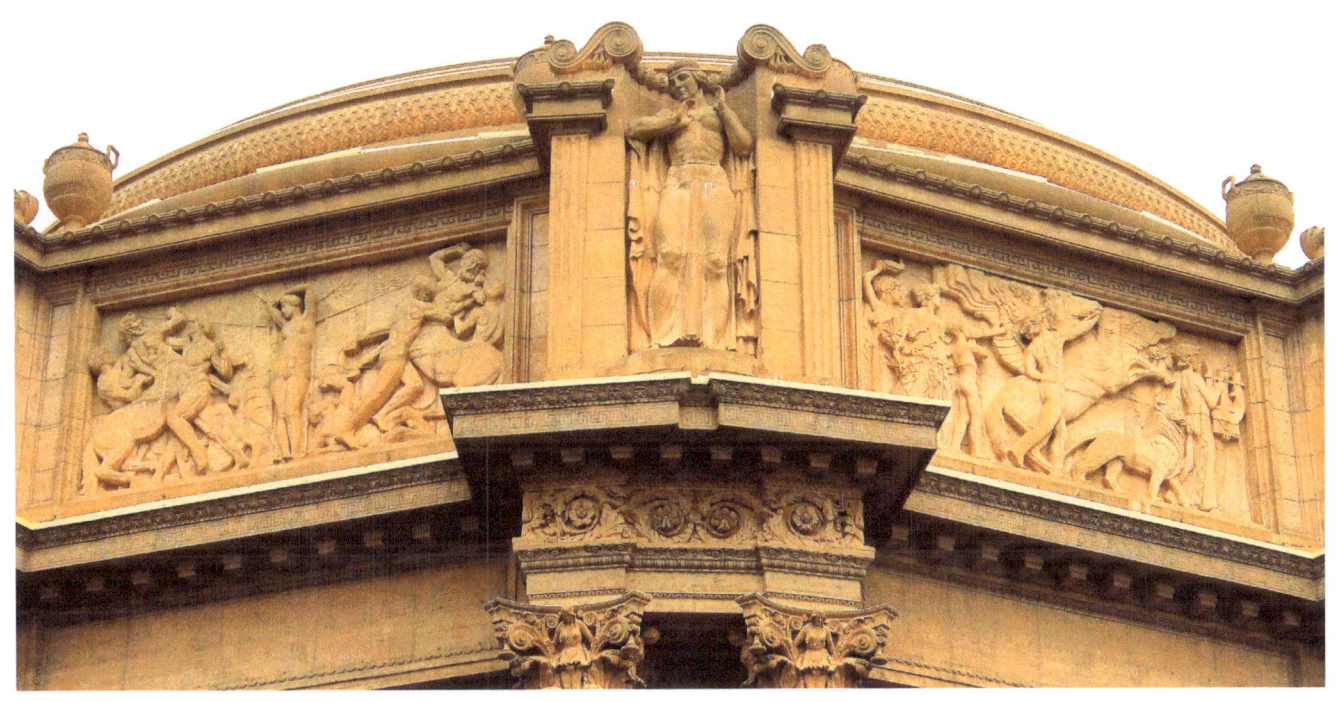

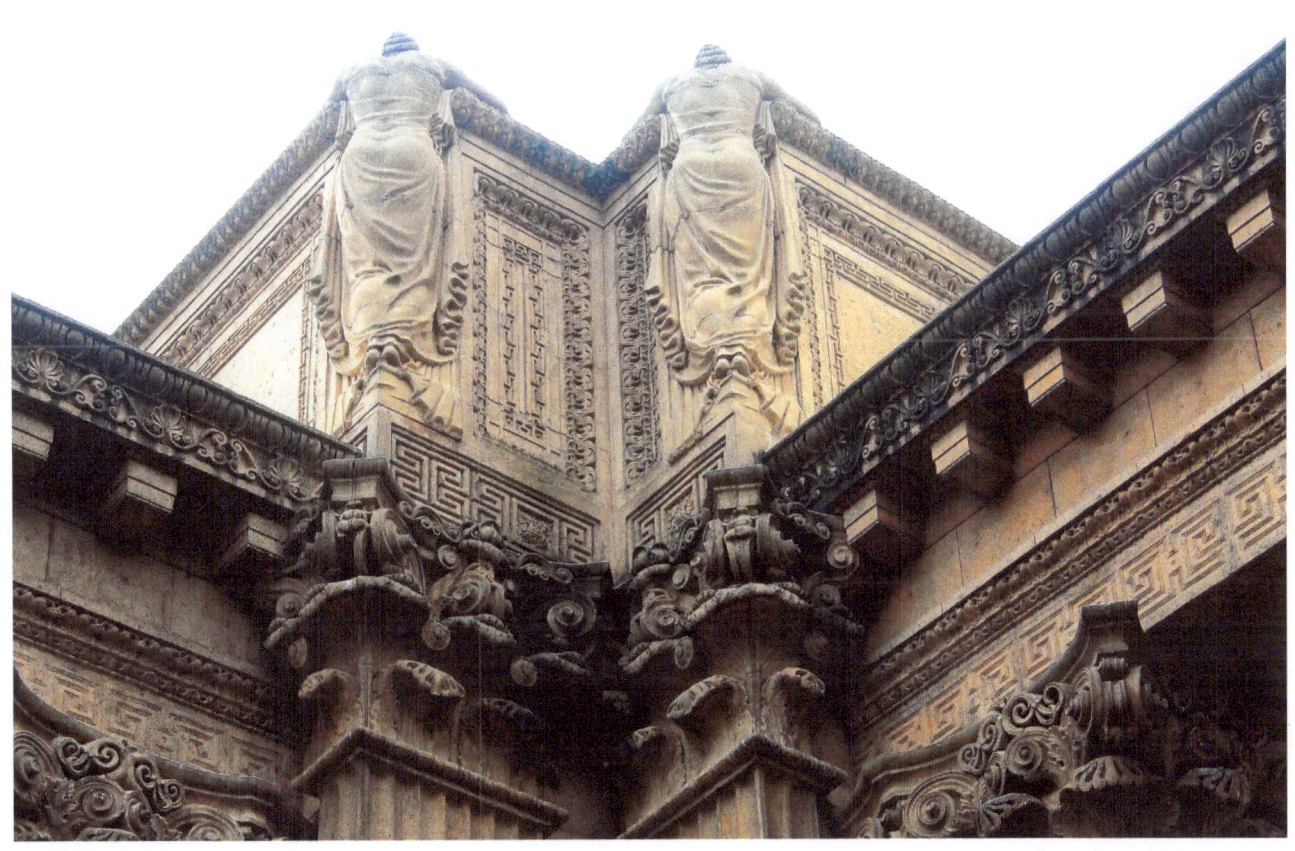

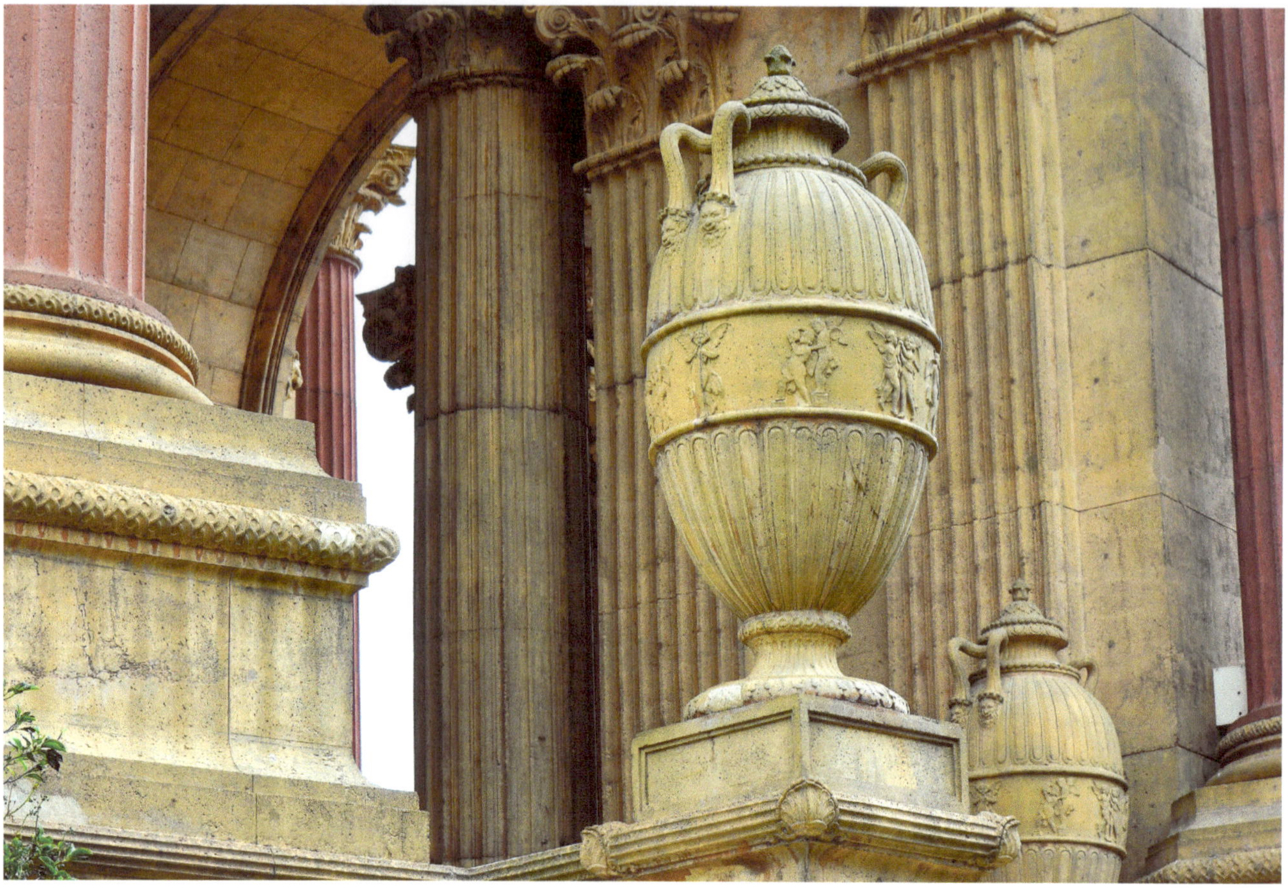

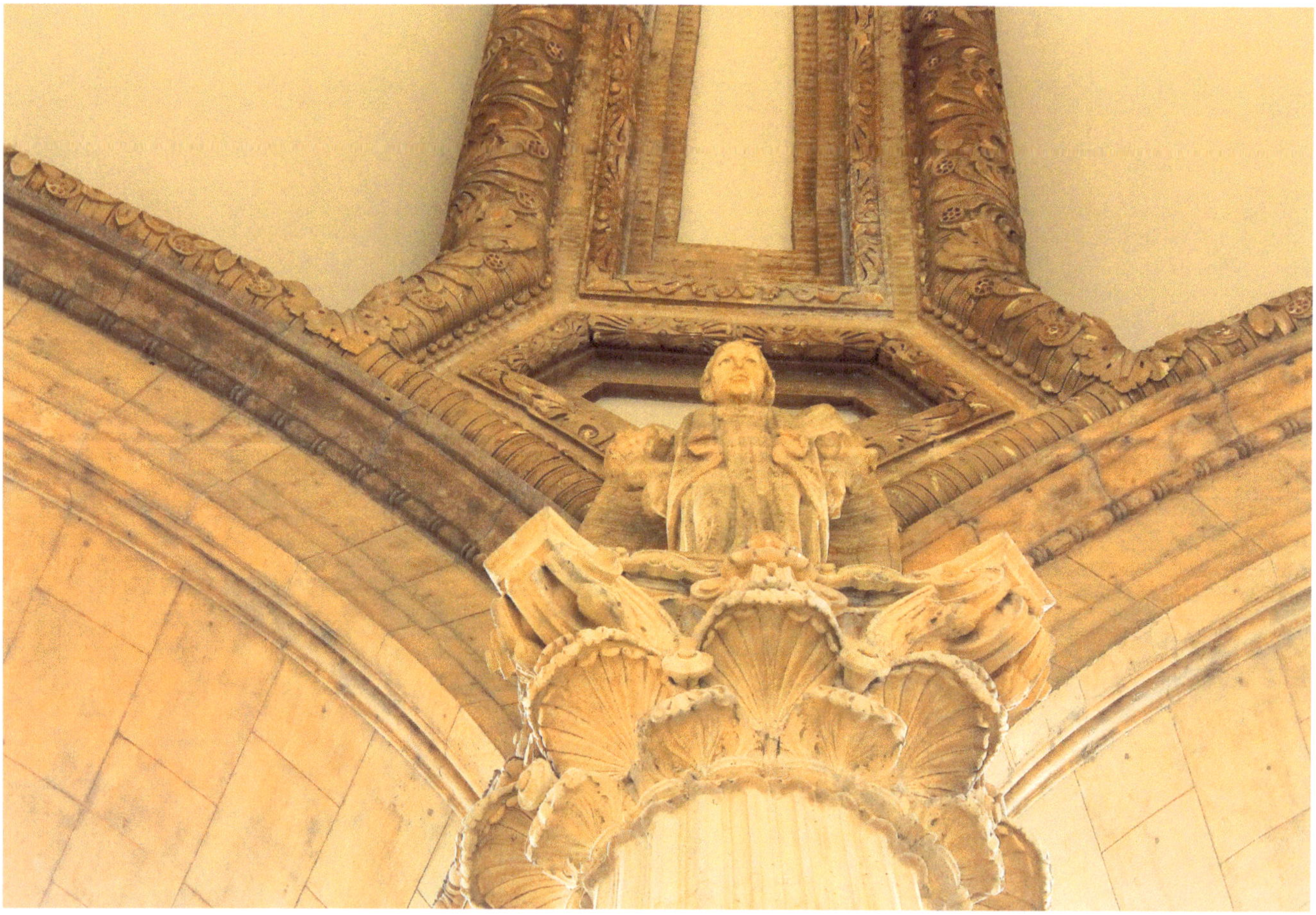

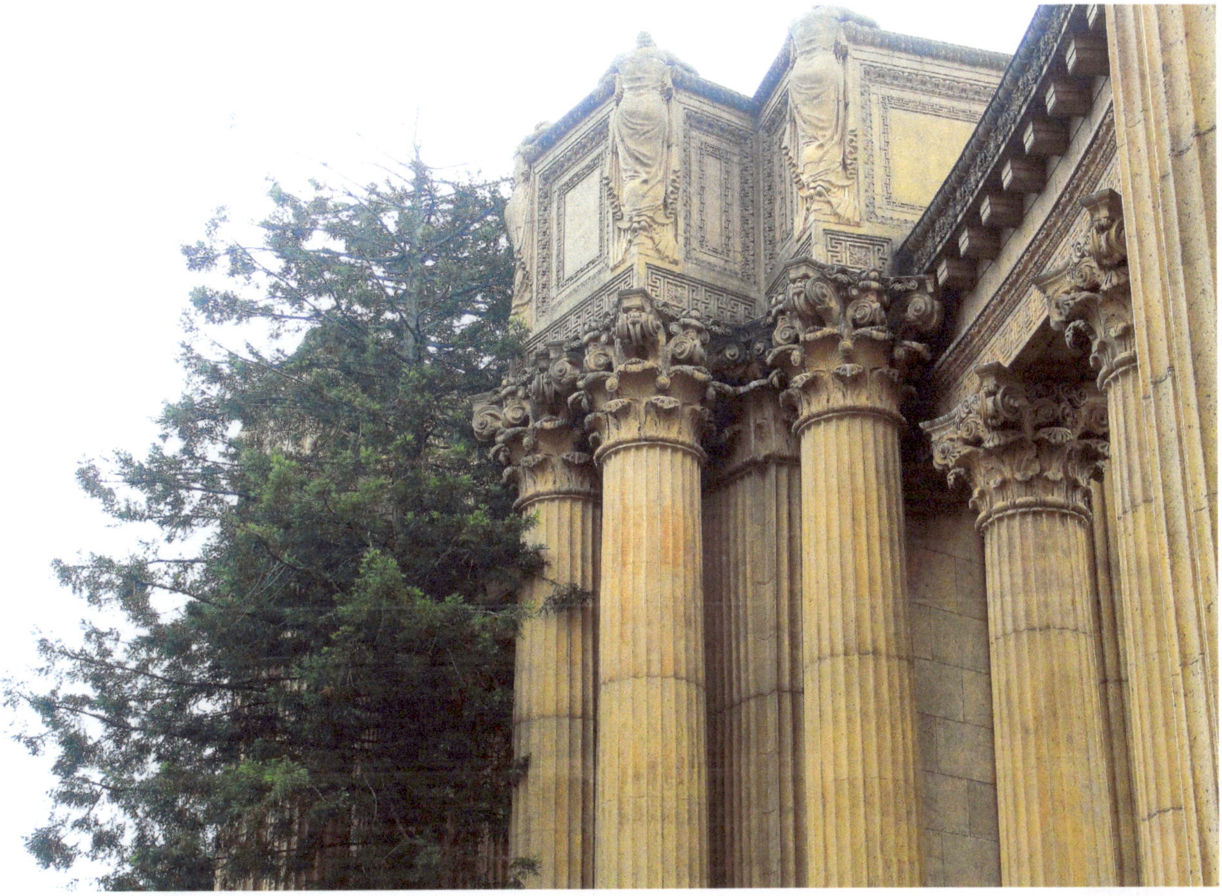

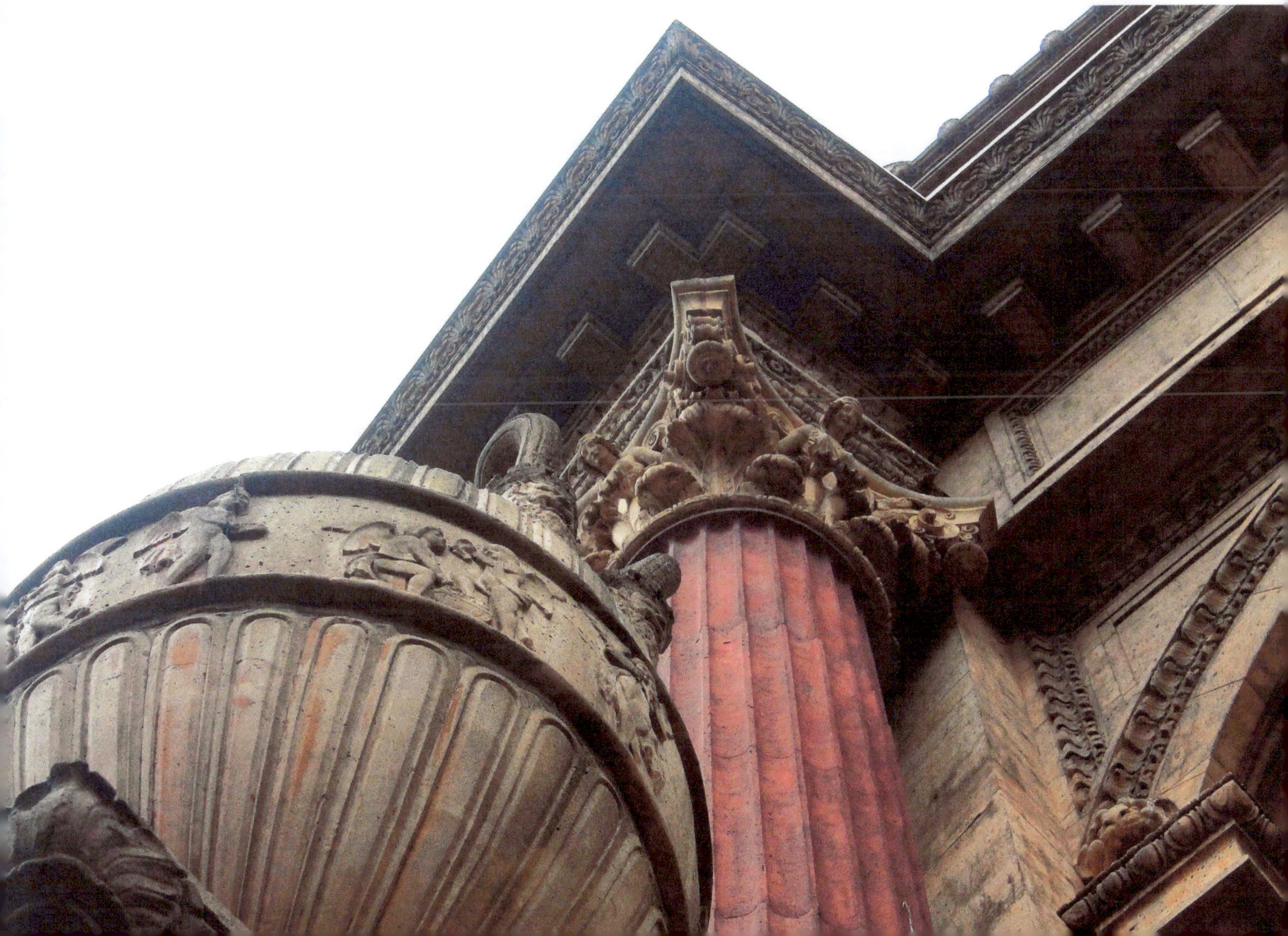

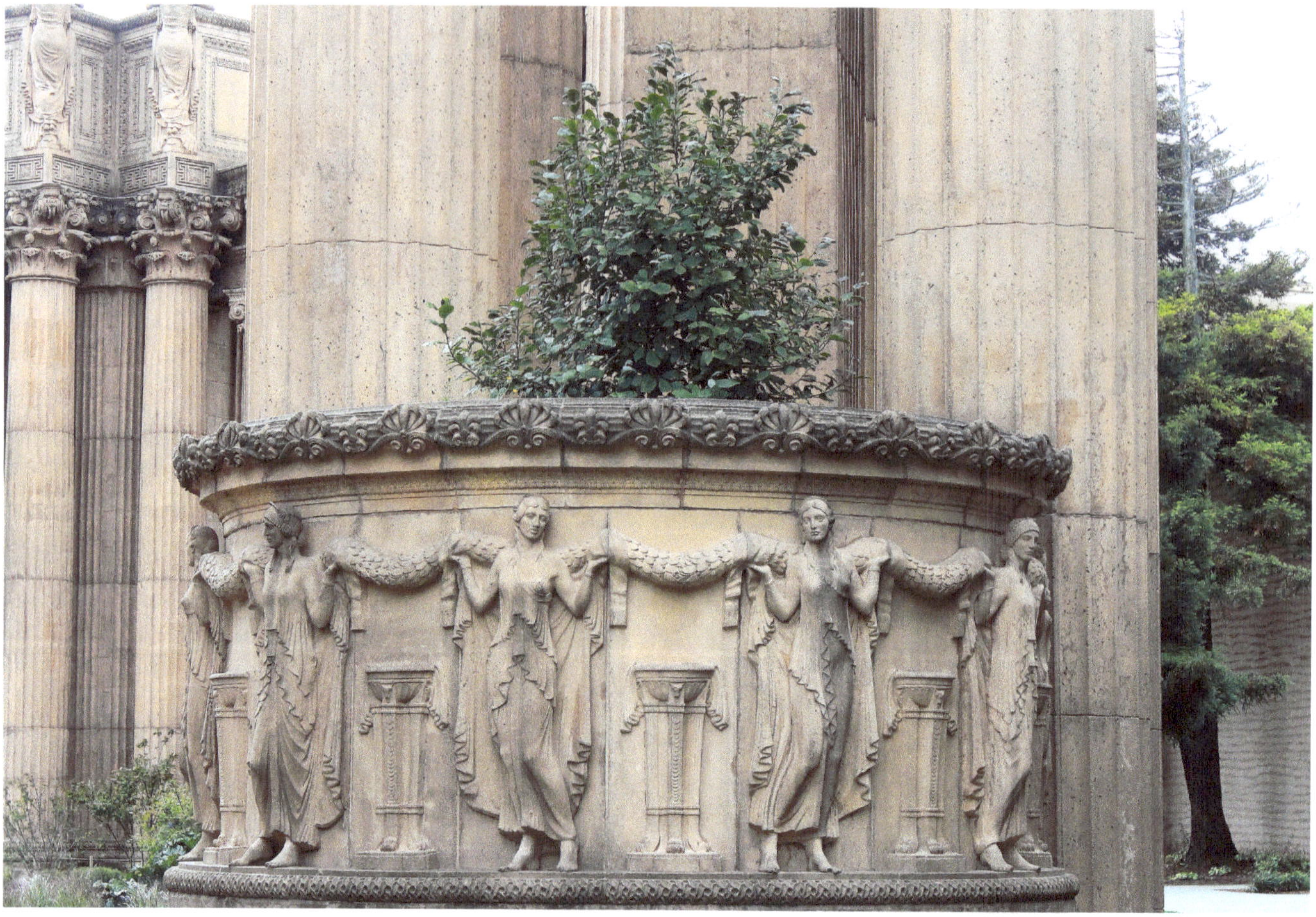

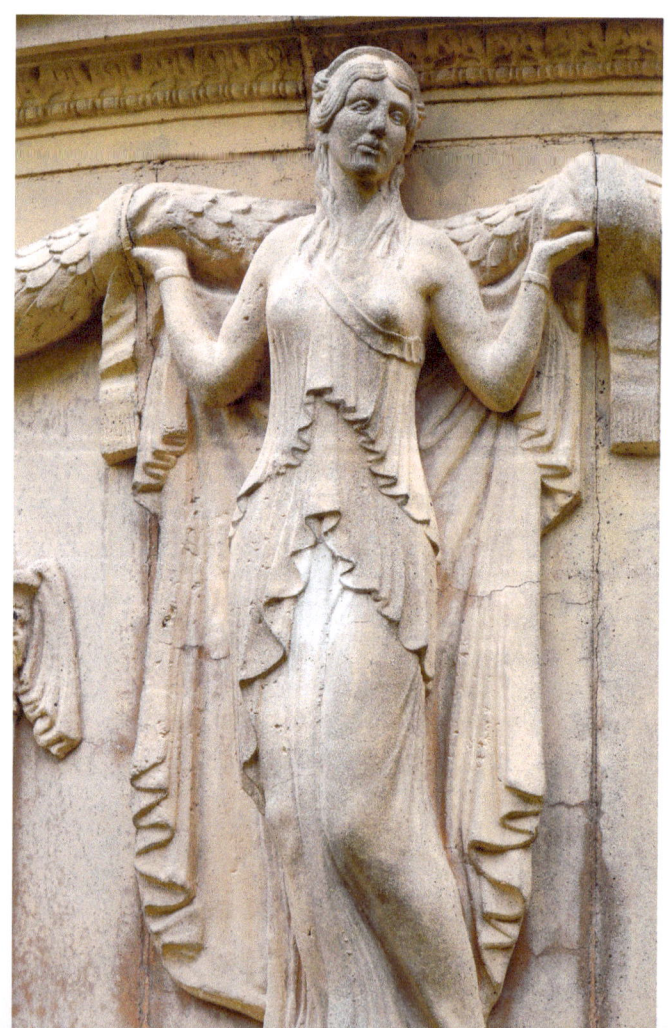

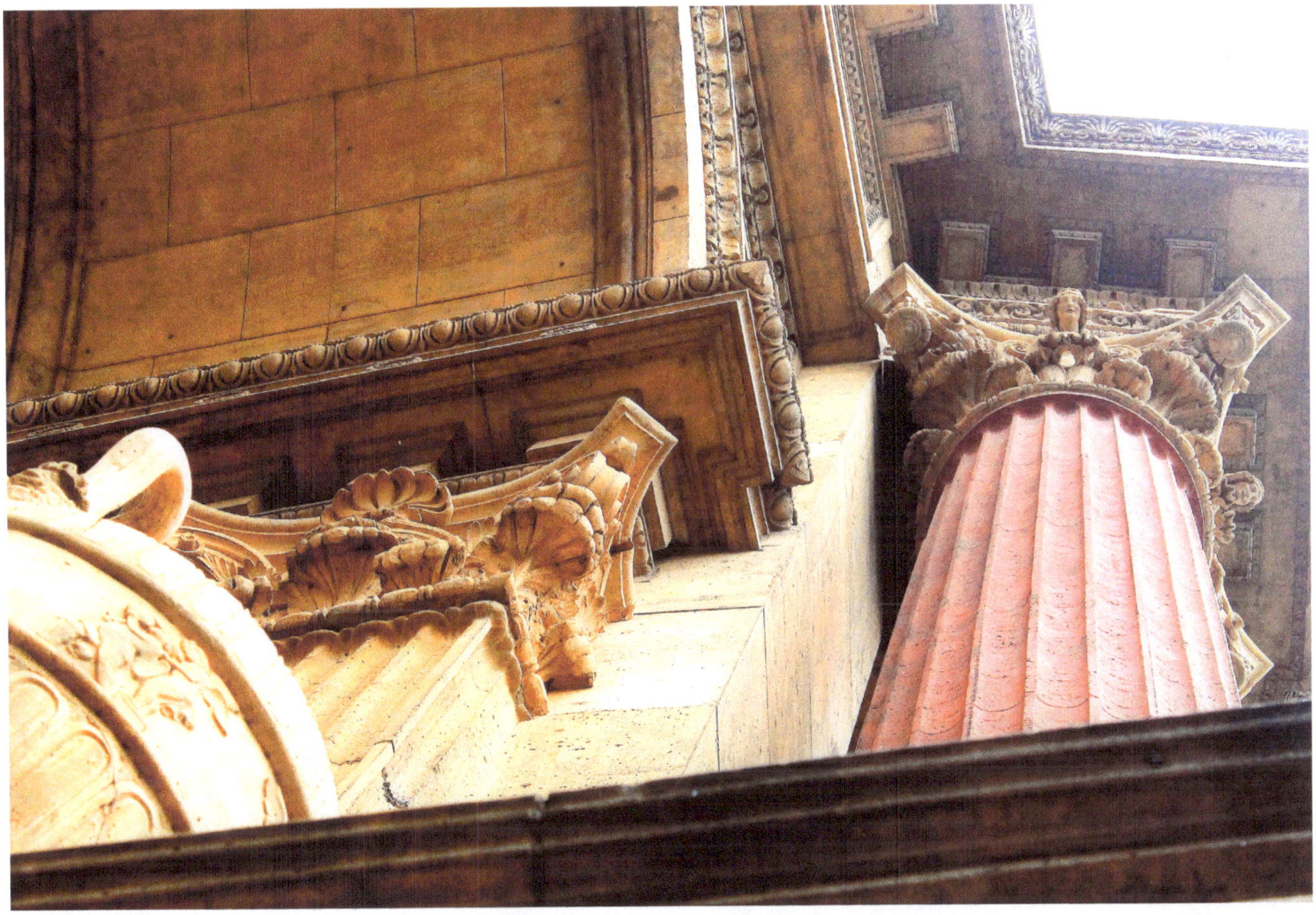

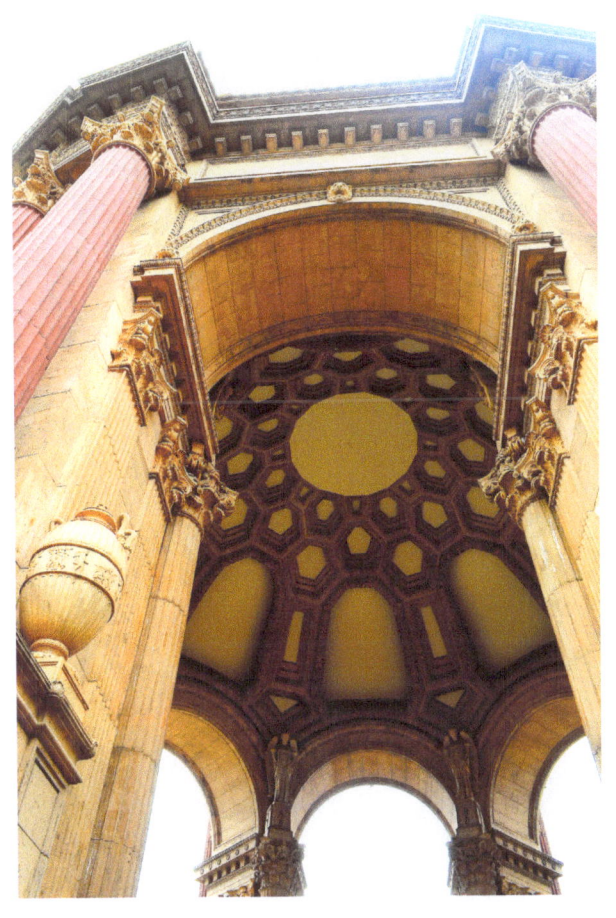

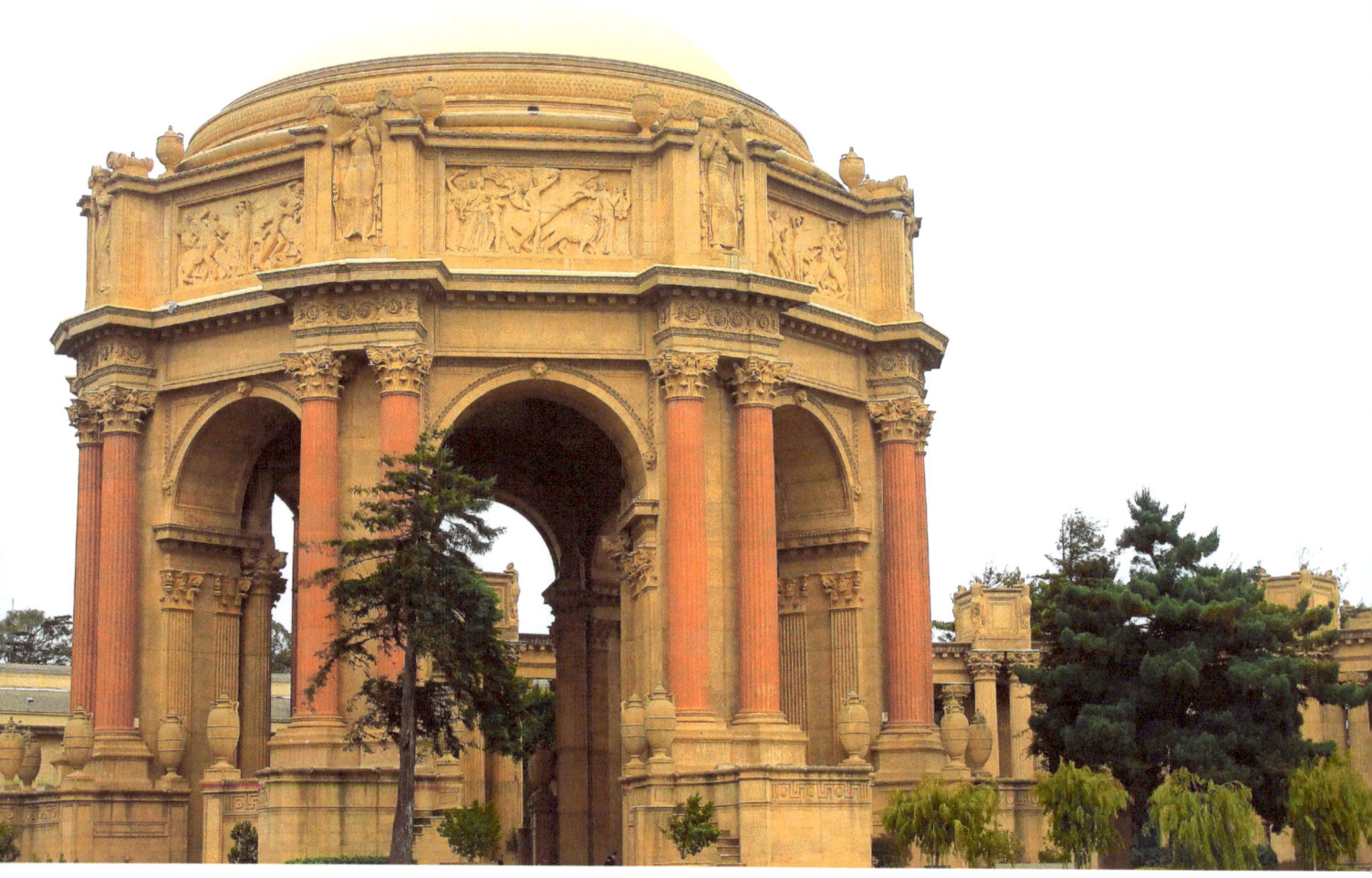

PALACE OF FINE ARTS

The Palace of Fine Arts was designed by Bernard Maybeck for the Panama-Pacific Exhibition in 1915. Maybeck was inspired by Greek and Roman architecture and used these influences in his design of the Palace. The original structure was intended to remain only until the end of the exposition, and as the years went on, it fell into a state of disrepair. In 1964 the original Palace of Fine Arts was torn down. Rebuilt in 1966, the Palace is now a permanent structure. It contains an exhibit hall and a central rotunda, as well as a pergola that extends 1,100 feet (340 meters) around it.

ERECTED BY
THE CITIZENS OF
SAN FRANCISCO
TO COMMEMORATE
THE VICTORY OF
THE AMERICAN NAVY
UNDER COMMODORE
GEORGE DEWEY AT
MANILA BAY MAY
FIRST MDCCCXCVIII

* * *

ON MAY TWENTY
THIRD MCMI THE
GROUND FOR THIS
MONUMENT WAS BRO-
KEN BY PRESIDENT
WILLIAM McKINLEY

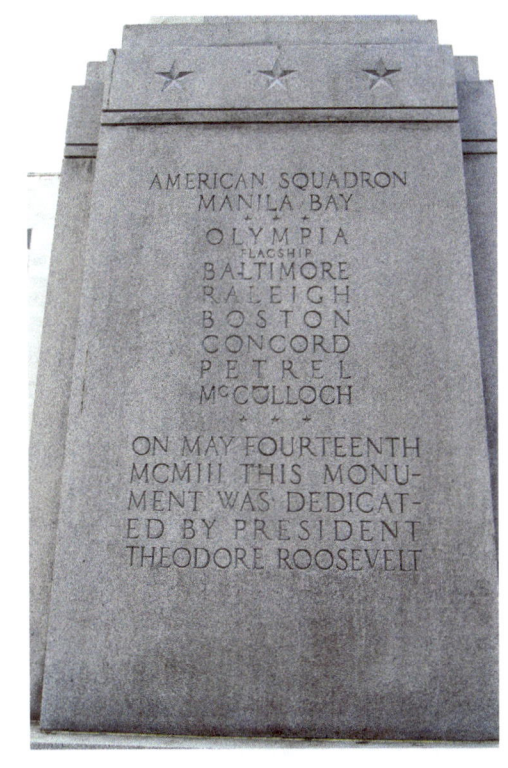

AMERICAN SQUADRON
MANILA BAY
* * *
OLYMPIA
FLAGSHIP
BALTIMORE
RALEIGH
BOSTON
CONCORD
PETREL
McCULLOCH
* * *

ON MAY FOURTEENTH
MCMIII THIS MONU-
MENT WAS DEDICAT-
ED BY PRESIDENT
THEODORE ROOSEVELT

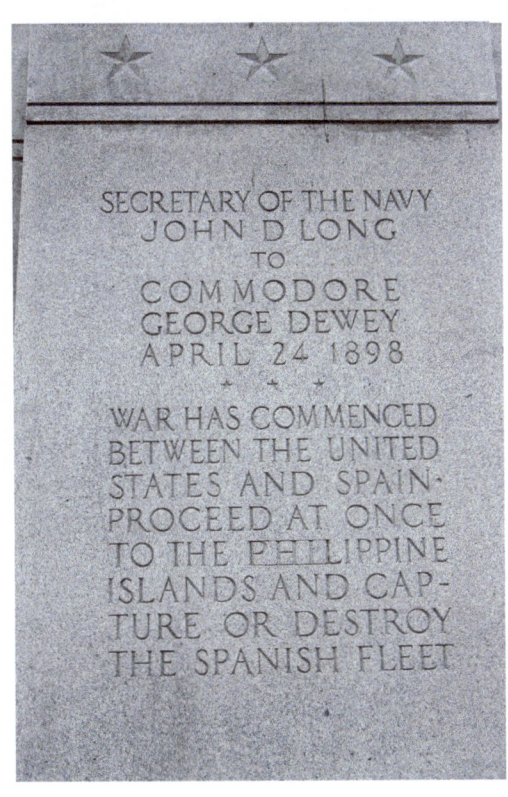

SECRETARY OF THE NAVY
JOHN D LONG
TO
COMMODORE
GEORGE DEWEY
APRIL 24 1898
* * *
WAR HAS COMMENCED
BETWEEN THE UNITED
STATES AND SPAIN·
PROCEED AT ONCE
TO THE PHILIPPINE
ISLANDS AND CAP-
TURE OR DESTROY
THE SPANISH FLEET

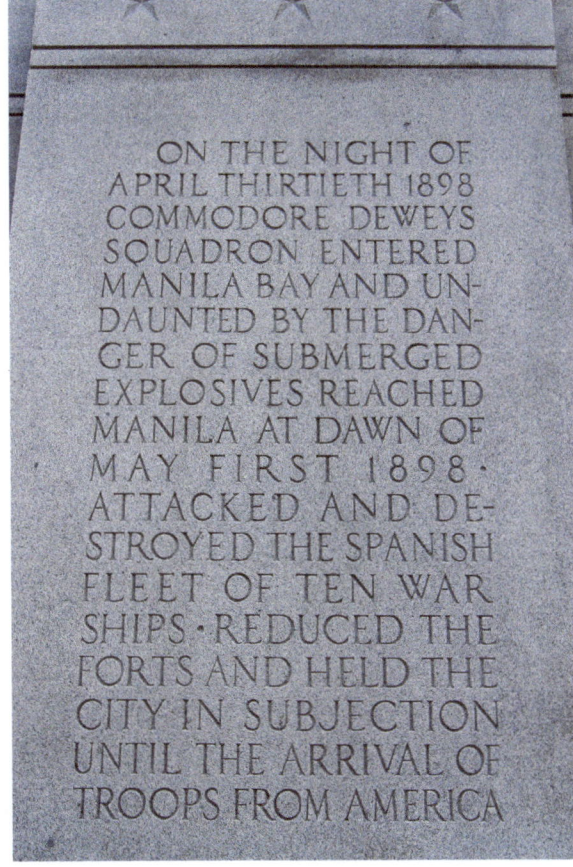

ON THE NIGHT OF
APRIL THIRTIETH 1898
COMMODORE DEWEYS
SQUADRON ENTERED
MANILA BAY AND UN-
DAUNTED BY THE DAN-
GER OF SUBMERGED
EXPLOSIVES REACHED
MANILA AT DAWN OF
MAY FIRST 1898·
ATTACKED AND DE-
STROYED THE SPANISH
FLEET OF TEN WAR
SHIPS·REDUCED THE
FORTS AND HELD THE
CITY IN SUBJECTION
UNTIL THE ARRIVAL OF
TROOPS FROM AMERICA

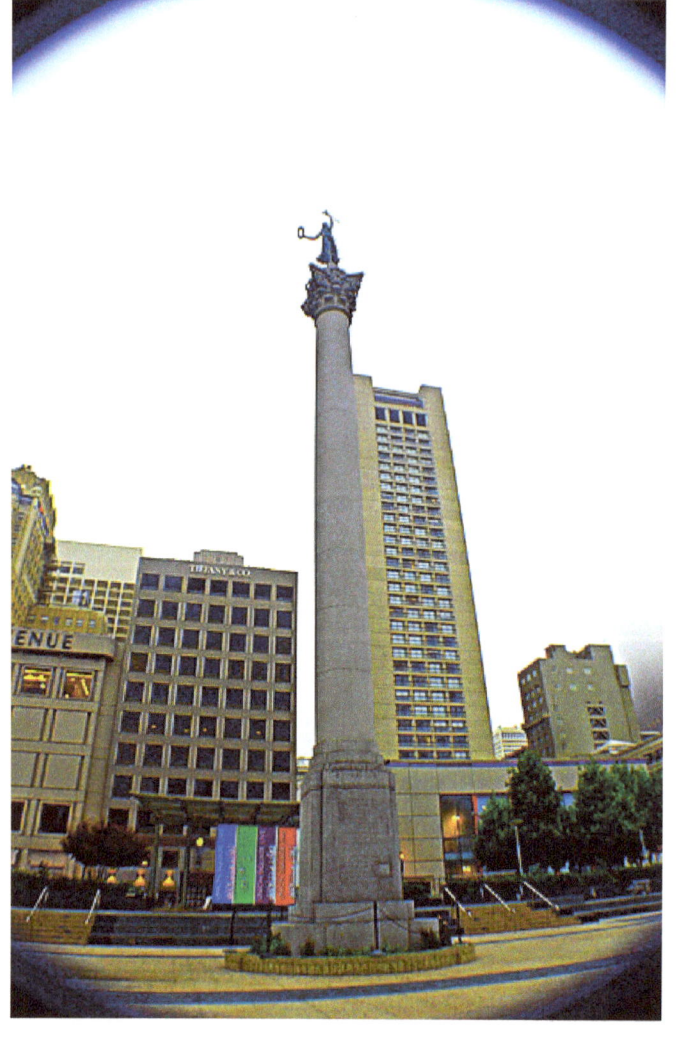

THE DEWEY MONUMENT

The Dewey Monument is located in Union Square, a 2.6 acre (1.05 hectare) square that got its name during the Civil War when it became a popular site for pro-Union rallies. The Dewey Monument was erected to honor Admiral George Dewey and the sailors of the United States Navy for their victory over the Spanish Navy at the Battle of Manila Bay during the Spanish-American War. Erected in 1903, the statue rises 95 feet (28.95 meters) above Union Square, the top of the statue features "Victory" modeled after San Francisco model Alma de Bretteville Spreckles.

SPECIAL DEDICATION TO JOEL CONKLIN

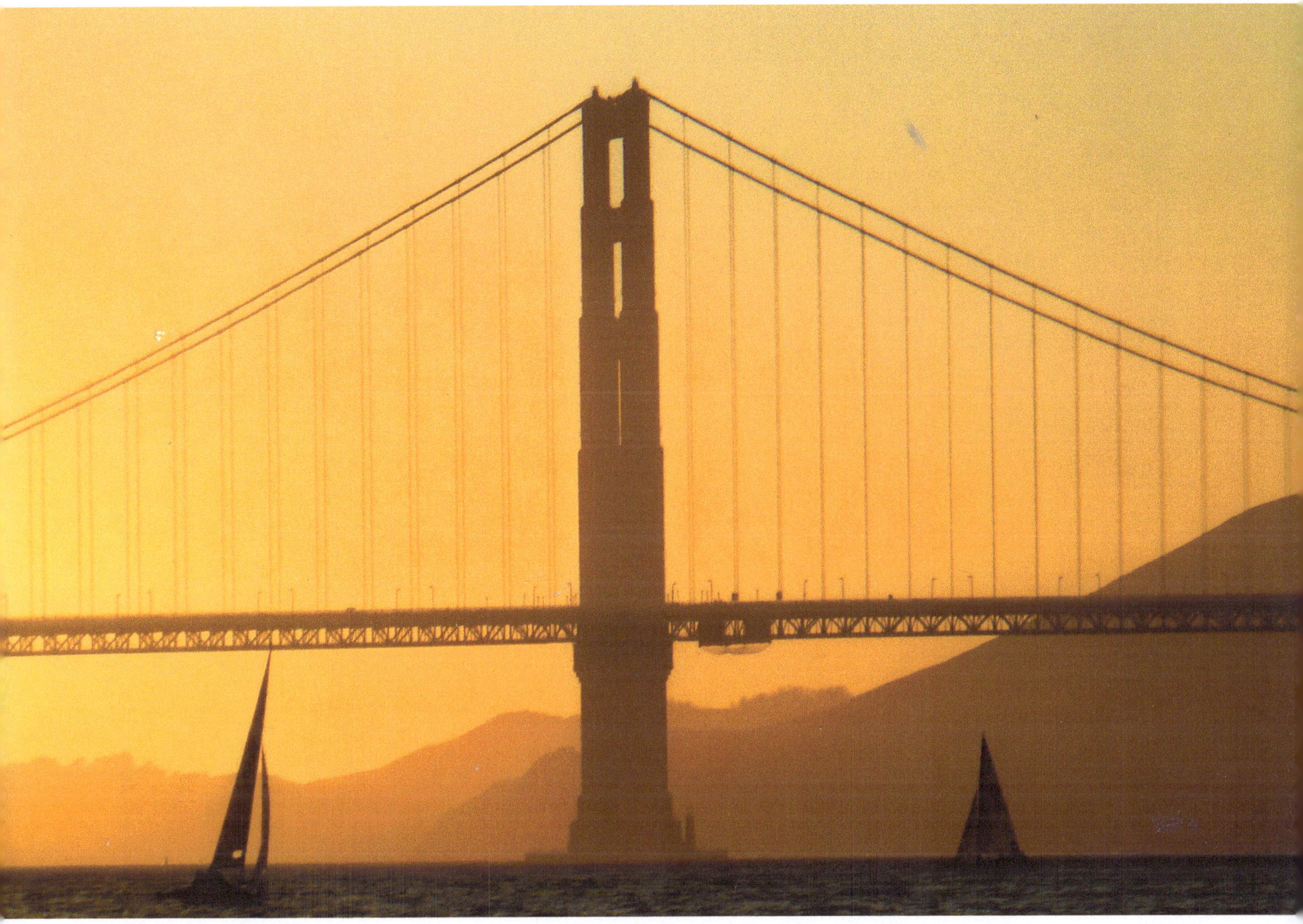

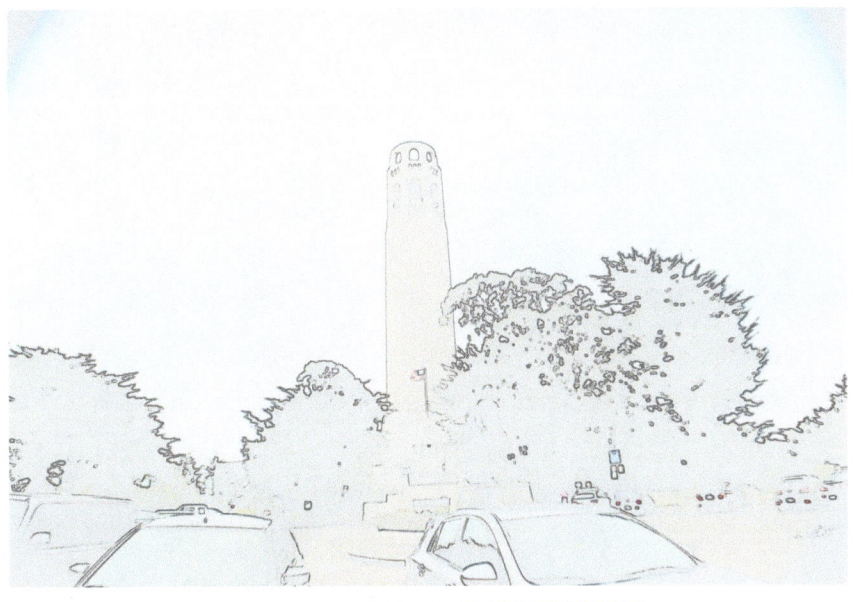

BY JOEL CONKLIN

SALVADORE NEWTON, EDITED BY JOEL CONKLIN

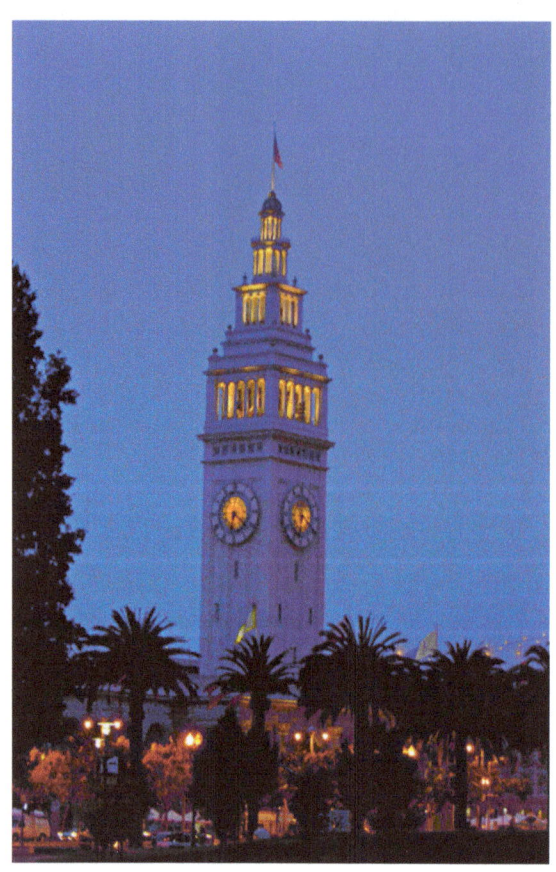

SALVADORE NEWTON, EDITED BY JOEL CONKLIN

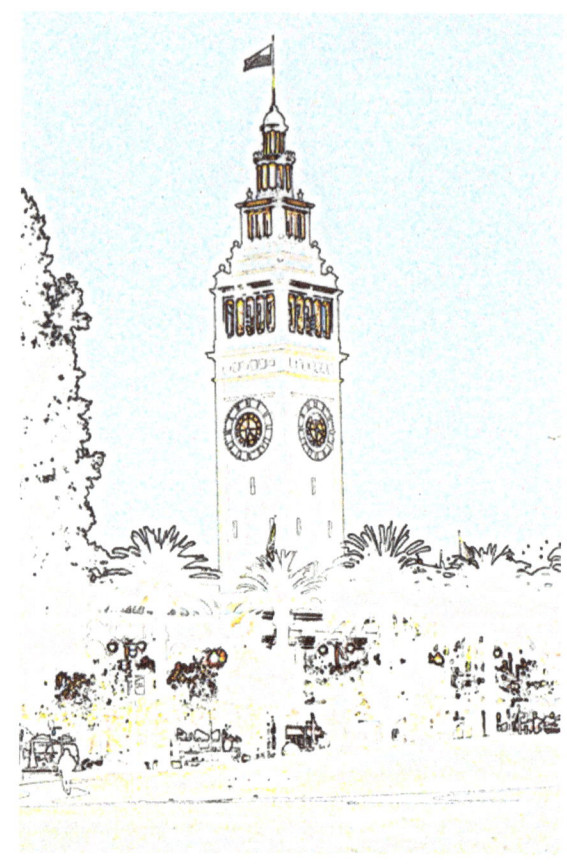

SALVADORE NEWTON, EDITED BY JOEL CONKLIN

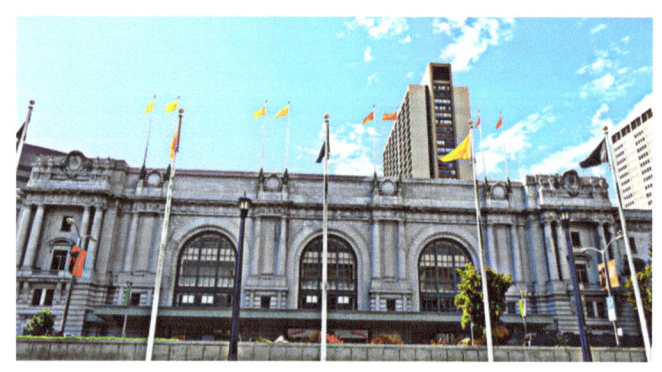

SALVADORE NEWTON, EDITED BY JOEL CONKLIN

BY JOEL CONKLIN

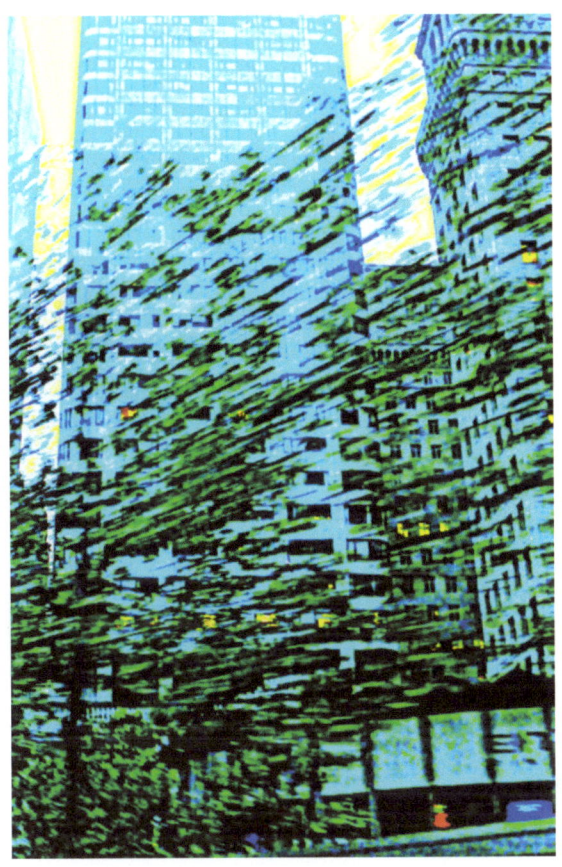

SALVADORE NEWTON, EDITED BY JOEL CONKLIN

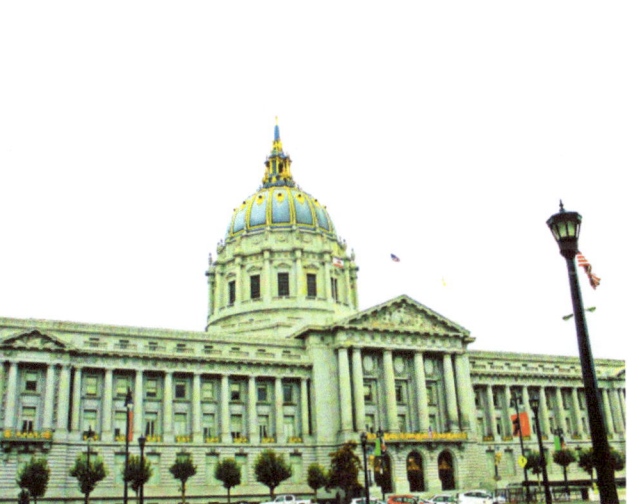

BY JOEL CONKLIN

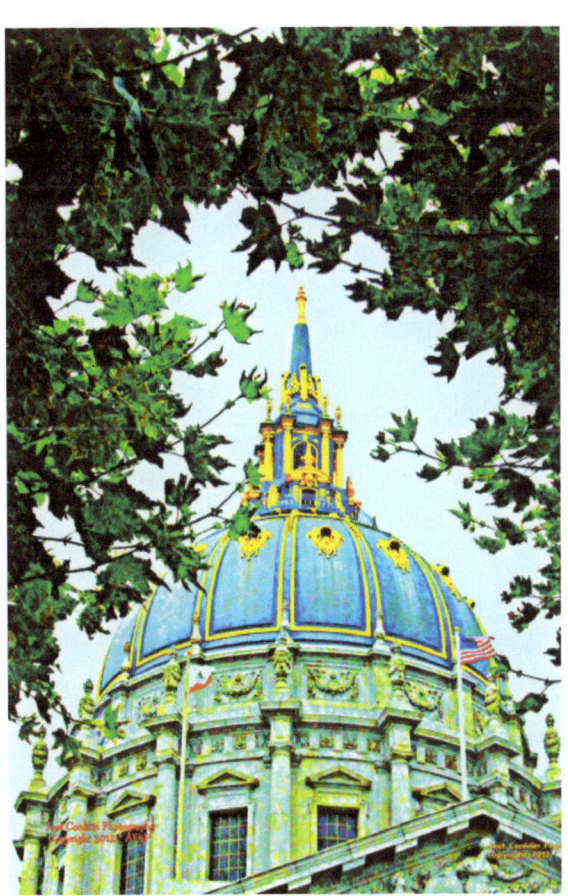

BY JOEL CONKLIN

BY JOEL CONKLIN

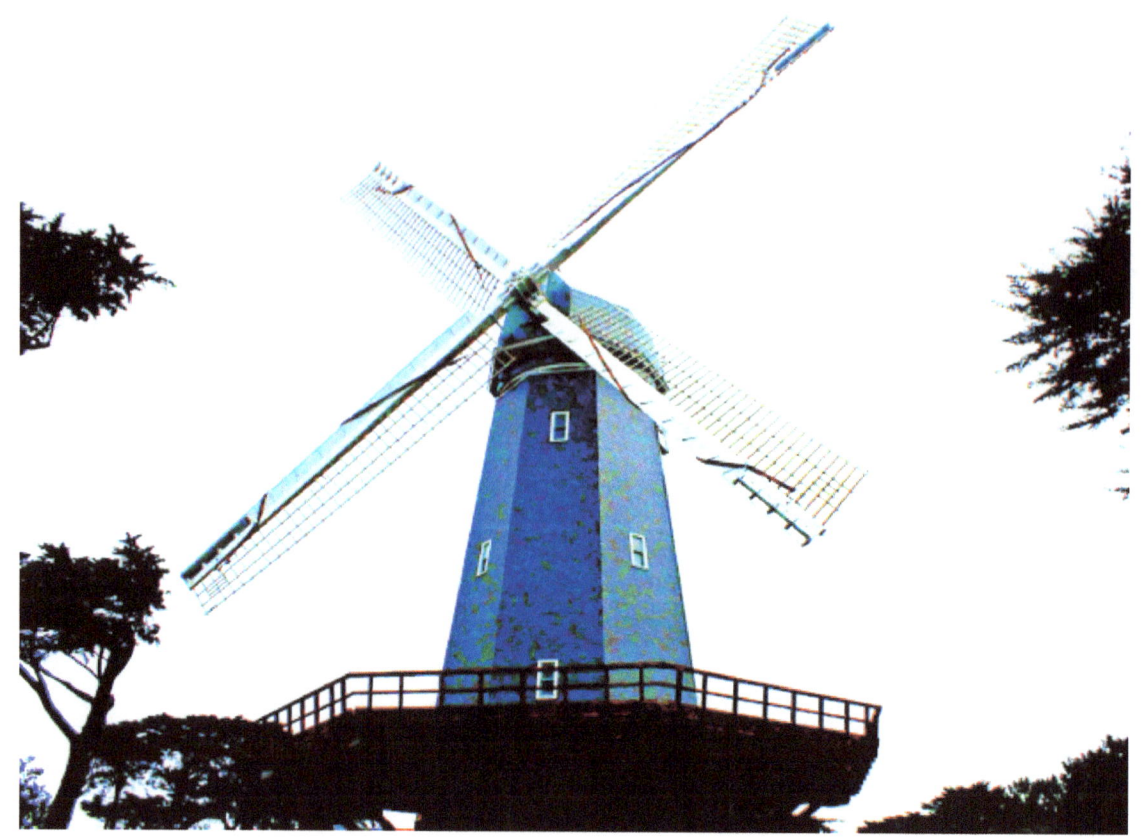

BY JOEL CONKLIN

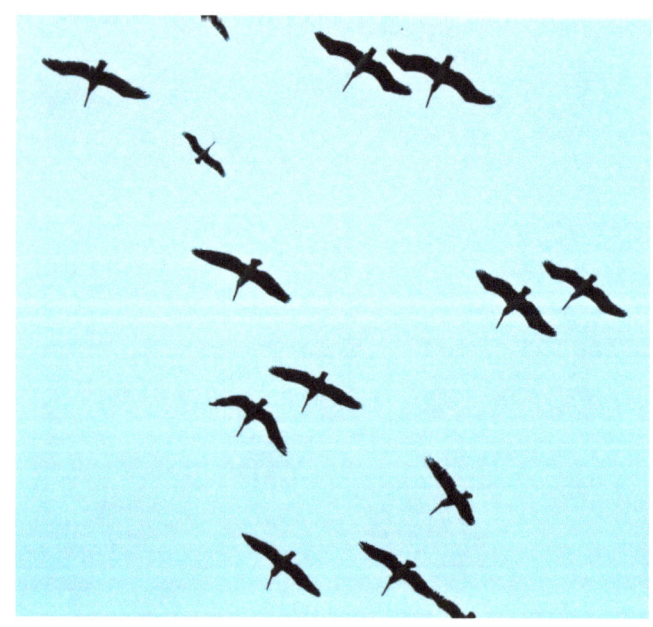

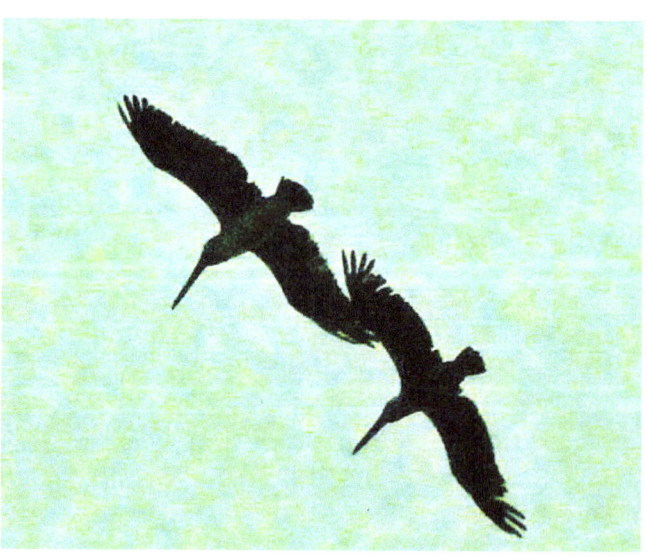

BY JOEL CONKLIN

BY JOEL CONKLIN

44

INDEX

SAN FRANCISCO: FROM THE GROUND UP

SOURCES

1.   "San Francisco City Hall", A View on Cities, 2013, accessed: 4/27/2013, www.aviewoncities.com/buildings/sf/sanfranciscocityhall.htm.

2.   Gregor Gosciniak "San Francisco City Hall", City Mayors, 06/26/2005, accessed: 04/27/13, www.citymayors.com/cityhalls/sanfrancisco_cityhall.html.

3.   "San Francisco City Hall Tour", San Francisco Arts Commission, accessed: 04/27/2013, www.sfartscommission.org/tours/CityHallVirtualTour.pdf.

4.   Stephen A. Worsley, "Coit Memorial Tower", 06/18/2007, accessed: 04/27/2013, pdfhost.focus.nps.gov/docs/NRHP/Text/07001468.pdf.

5.   "Transamerica Pyramid", Emporis, 2012, accessed: 04/27/2013, www.emporis.com/building/transamericapyramid-sanfrancisco-ca-usa.

6.   "Pyramid Facts and Figures", Transamerica, 2013, accessed: 04/28/2013, www.transamerica.com/about_us/about_the_pyramid/pyramid_facts_and_figures.asp.

7.   "The Mark Hopkins Hotel", Emporis, 2012, accessed: 04/27/2013, www.emporis.com/building/the-mark-hopkins-hotel-san-francisco-ca-usa.

8.   "Mark Hopkins Hotel", City Walking Guide, accessed: 05/06/2013, www.citywalkingguide.com/sanfrancisco/markhopkins.

9.   "555 California Street", Emporis, 2012, accessed: 05/06/2013, www.emporis.com/building/555californiastreet-sanfrancisco-ca-usa.

10.   "555 California Street", City Profile, accessed: 05/06/2013, www.cityprofile.com/california/555-california-street.html.

11.   "About 555", Vornado Realty Trust, 2013, accessed: 05/06/2013, www.555cal.com/about/building-features.

12.   "Museum History", Asian Art Museum, 2013, accessed: 05/06/2013, www.asianart.org/about/history.

13.   Kyle Mizokami "Murphy Windmill Reopens In Golden Gate Park", Ocean Beach Bulletin, 04/28/2012, accessed: 05/07/2013, HTTP://oceanbeachbulletin.com/2012/04/28/murphy-windmill-reopens-in-golden-gate-park/.

14.   "Mision San Francisco de Asis", Mission Dolores, 2007-2013, accessed: 05/07/2013, missiondolores.org/old-mission/visitor.html.

15.   "The San Francisco Ferry Building Clock", SF City Guides, accessed: 05/07/2013, www.sfcityguides.org/public_guidelines.html?srch_text=dorian+clairHYPERLINK "http://www.sfcityguides.org/public_guidelines.html?srch_text=dorian+clair&submit=Search&submitted2=True"&HYPERLINK "http://www.sfcityguides.org/public_guidelines.html?srch_text=dorian+clair&submit=Search&submitted2=True"submit=SearchHYPERLINK "http://www.sfcityguides.org/public_guidelines.html?srch_text=dorian+clair&submit=Search&submitted2=True"&HYPERLINK "http://www.sfcityguides.org/public_guidelines.html?srch_text=dorian+clair&submit=Search&submitted2=True"submitted2=True.

16.   "Ferry Building History", Ferry Building Marketplace, 2005, accessed: 05/07/2013, www.ferry-buildingmarketplace.com/history.php.

17.   "Fairmont Hotel", Emporis, 2000-2012, accessed: 05/08/2013, www.emporis.com/building/fairmonthotel-sanfrancisco-ca-usa952.

18.   "Fairmont Hotel Tower", Emporis, 2000-2012, accessed: 05/08/2013, www.emporis.com/building/fairmont-hotel-tower-san-francisco-ca-usa.

19.   "Dining", The Fairmont San Francisco, 2013, accessed: 05/08/2013, www.fairmont.com/san-francisco/dining/.

20.   "Construction Timeline Golden Gate Bridge December 1932 to April 1937", Golden Gate Bridge, 2006-2012, accessed: 05/12/2013, goldengatebridge.org/research/ConstructionTimeline.php.

21.   "Key Dates", Golden Gate Bridge, 2006-2012, accessed: 05/12/2013, goldengatebridge.org/research/dates.php.

22.   "Bridge Design and Construction Statistics", Golden Gate Bridge, 2006-2012, accessed: 05/12/2013, goldengatebridge.org/research/factsGGBdesign.php.

23.   "The Strauss Team", Golden Gate Bridge, 2006-2012, accessed: 05/12/2013, goldengatebridge.org/research/StraussTeam.php.

24.   "One Embarcadero Center", Emporis, 2000-2012, accessed: 05/13/2013, www.emporis.com/building/one-embarcadero-center-san-francisco-ca-usa.

25.   "Two Embarcadero Center", Emporis, 2000-2012, accessed: 05/13/2013, www.emporis.com/building/two-embarcadero-center-san-francisco-ca-usa.

26.   "Three Embarcadero Center", Emporis, 2000-2012, accessed: 05/13/2013, www.emporis.com/building/three-embarcadero-center-san-francisco-ca-usa.

27. "Four Embarcadero Center", Emporis, 2000-2012, accessed: 05/13/2013, www.emporis.com/building/four-embarcadero-center-san-francisco-ca-usa.

28. "Hyatt Regency San Francisco", Emporis, 2000-2012, accessed: 05/13/2013, www.emporis.com/building/hyattregencysanfrancisco-sanfrancisco-ca-usa.

29. "Le Meridien San Francisco", Emporis, 2000-2012, accessed: 05/13/2013, www.emporis.com/building/le-meridien-san-francisco-san-francisco-ca-usa.

30. "Embarcadero West", Emporis, 2000-2012, accessed: 05/13/2013, www.emporis.com/building/embarcaderowest-sanfrancisco-ca-usa.

31. "About", Embarcadero Center, 2013, accessed: 05/13/2013, embarcaderocenter.com/about/.

32. "Fact Sheet", Westin ST Francis Groups, accessed: 05-27-2013, www.westinstfrancisgroups.com/planner/assets/documents/WSF_Fact_Sheet.pdf.

33. "The Westin ST Francis", Emporis, 2000-2012, accessed: 05/27/2013, www.emporis.com/building/the-westin-st-francis-san-francisco-ca-usa.

34. "The Westin ST Francis Tower", Emporis, 2000-2012, accessed: 05/27/2013, www.emporis.com/building/the-westin-st-francis-tower-san-francisco-ca-usa.

35. "Cathedral History and Art", Grace Cathedral, 2013, accessed: 05/27/2013, www.gracecathedral.org/visit/cathedral-history-art/.

36. "The Highlights of The Cathedral Structure", Grace Cathedral, 2013, accessed: 05/27/2013, www.gracecathedral.org/visit/cathedral-tour/.

37. "Tower History", Sutro Tower, 2000-2013, accessed: 05/27/2013, sutrotower.com/about-the-tower/history/.

38. "The Palace of Fine Arts", Exploratorium, 1998, accessed: 05/28/2013, www.exploratorium.edu/history/palace/.

39. "Rebuilding", Exploratorium, 1998, accessed: 05/28/2013, www.exploratorium.edu/history/palace/palace_4.html.

40. "Rebuilding", Exploratorium, 1998, accessed: 05/28/2013, www.exploratorium.edu/history/palace/palace_5.html.

41. "Preservation", Exploratorium, 1998, accessed: 05/28/2013, www.exploratorium.edu/history/palace/palace_3.html.

42. James Yu, "Palace of Fine Arts", University of Maryland, 2005, accessed: 05/28/2013, http://hdl.handle.net/1903.1/18.

43. "Union Square-Dewey Monument", Art and Architecture-San Francisco, 2012, accessed: 05/29/2013, www.artandarchitecture-sf.com//union-square-san-francisco-march-26-2012.html.

44. "Union Square", A View on Cities, 2013, accessed: 05/30/2013, www.aviewoncities.com/sf/union-square.htm.

45. "Dewey Monument", Emporis, 2012, accessed: 05/30/2013, www.emporis.com/building/dewey-monument-san-francisco-ca-usa.